EXPLORERS OF HUMANKIND

MOSHE FELDENKRAIS

ALEXANDER LOWEN

IDA ROLF

CHARLOTTE SELVER & CHARLES BROOKS

BARBARA BROWN

ASHLEY MONTAGU

KARL PRIBRAM

CARL ROGERS

MARGARET MEAD

1817 Published in San Francisco by

EXPLORERS
OF
HUMANKIND.

Edited, with Introduction and Biographical Notes by

THOMAS HANNA

HARPER & ROW, PUBLISHERS
New York, Hagerstown, San Francisco, London

EXPLORERS OF HUMANKIND. Copyright © 1979 by Thomas
Hanna. All rights reserved. Printed in the United States of America. No
part of this book may be used or reproduced in any manner whatsoever
without written permission except in the case of brief quotations
embodied in critical articles and reviews. For information address Harper
& Row, Publishers, Inc., 10 East 53rd Street, New York, NY 10022.
Published simultaneously in Canada by Fitzhenry & Whiteside, Limited,
Toronto.

FIRST EDITION

Designed by Jim Mennick

Library of Congress Cataloging in Publication Data

Main entry under title:

EXPLORERS OF HUMANKIND

Includes bibliographies.
1. Humanistic psychology. 2. Mind and body. 3. Personality. 4. Personality
and culture. I. Feldenkrais, Moshé, 1904– II. Hanna, Tomas, 1928–
BF204.V57   1979   128   78-65664
ISBN 0-06-250375-8

79 80 81 82 83 10 9 8 7 6 5 4 3 2 1

Contents

About This Book

I cannot imagine how there could be more power and fascination than that which is packed into this small volume. The power and fascination stem from two sources. The first of these sources, very obviously, is the ten extraordinary men and women who accepted my invitation to write this book. The second source is the simple and profound theme about which they have written: What is the nature of the human being?

In the first instance, these ten scientists and healers are exemplary in being responsible for some of this century's most extraordinary advances in understanding how human beings function and how they function best: how they can best be healed, how they can best maintain their health and how they can expand that health even further into exceptional creativity, efficiency and fulfillment.

In the second instance, this book provides us with the great fortune of having some of the leading scientists and healers of the twentieth century share with us their vision of what human nature is.

This vision is, in each case, a healing vision. It is a hopeful and optimistic vision, framed within a broad-ranging scientific perspective that allows us to understand how it is that humans function best. In particular, this is a somatic perspective:

Namely, it is a viewpoint that pays homage to the bodily life of humankind.

This is a book about science, it is a book about ourselves as human beings, and it is a book about human healing, human health and human wholeness. In sum, it is a book that presents the healing vision of this century's most visionary healers.

T.H.

Introduction: The Sphinx and the Soma

The Sphinx was a winged creature with the head of a woman, the body of a lion and a devastating riddle that no one in Thebes could answer—not, at least, until Oedipus came along.

The riddle was this: What is it that has one voice and yet becomes four-footed and two-footed and three-footed? An incorrect answer led to dire consequences: One was eaten alive. A large portion of the Theban population was consumed before the riddle was solved. Only one creature in all the world could have such contradictory traits: the human creature, who in infancy crawls on all fours; in adulthood, on two legs; and in old age hobbles along with the help of a cane. The wisdom of Oedipus lay in his realization that the human being was the most complex of all creatures.

The riddle of the human being is still with us, but the nature of the human animal has turned out to be infinitely more complex than it seemed to be when the Sphinx roamed the mythical lands of antique Greece. During the twentieth century we have learned an immense amount about ourselves, *Homo sapiens*. The vast data accumulated by biology, physiology and the behavioral sciences have, like so many dots in a *pointillist* painting, begun to form a coherent picture. The complexity has taken on a shape, and it is the same shape first envisaged by Darwin and Wallace: that of a genetically ancient animal whose bodily appearance is the result of a long series of functional adaptations that have enhanced its survival.

Research during this century—in biology, ethology, biochemistry, et al.—has narrowed the gap that was once thought to exist between the human animal and the other three million or more species of animals inhabiting the earth. Nonhuman animals were discovered to have far more "human" traits than was hitherto known, and humans were found to be much more "animal" than our separatist pride allowed us to believe. Even as the Copernican revolution forced us to realize that the earth was not the center of the solar system, the Darwinian revolution forced us to recognize that humans were not an absolutely unique species of the animal kingdom, but rather one of its many offshoots. Gradually the picture emerged: lurking behind the self-conscious, language-using, symbol-loving human was an infinitely clever and ancient animal whose functional roots led downward into the great depths of biological history.

We are twigs on the branch of a colossal tree, and we are now learning to see ourselves more transparently in our biological depths. The way our bodies look and the ways our bodies function are, like the outer skin of an onion, later layers that have been laminated onto earlier and similar biological layers.

That a fin, a webbed foot, a wing, a paw and a hand are all structurally similar was already obvious by the eighteenth century and was reflected homologically in that century's classification of the entire animal kingdom. What Charles Darwin added to that static classification was time: biological history which, like a needle, threaded its way through the classification charts, linking and making historical sense of these similar layers. But by turning biology into biological history, Darwin also gave a grand theme to that historical continuum: survival. Every new wrinkle that emerged along this evolutionary continuum—be it a longer tail, a sharper fang or a stronger leg—evolved because it was a functional improvement over what had gone before. A new difference, a new layer, a new species, always succeeded in establishing itself because of its improved chances for survival.

Thus, the standard way modern biology looks at different bodily structures is always to ask: What is it for? What function does it serve for the purpose of better survival? This is to say that we have increasingly turned our attention to the *bodies* of animals, human or otherwise. We are no longer, as in the eighteenth century, viewing them as different structures, but instead, we are looking *through the structure* at the different ways different bodies function. This way of observing and studying animals—human or otherwise—is *somatic*, and it is the basic point of view reflected in the nine remarkable essays contained in this volume.

The word somatic is derived from the Greek word *soma*, which means the living body. In biological and physiological usage the term somatic refers to the essential, genetic body—the core of structure and functions that is genetically passed on from generation to generation. This is to say that a soma is not simply a "body" in the sense of being merely a physical structure; a soma is a functioning body, a living body. All animals—human or otherwise—are somas, and any soma of any species of the animal kingdom is a specific body of functions.

Here we encounter a curious paradox: A somatic viewpoint focuses on the body of a living creature in order to see its functions. The movements of the bodily structure are the expressions of its way of functioning. The more a somatic scientist looks at a living body, the less he sees the structure, and the more he sees the functions. It is almost as if a somatic scientist is seeking to discover the same thing sought by the psychologist, namely, the principles of a living being's behavior. This is curious in that whereas in human psychology the traditional concern has been to understand bodily behavior in terms of the human psyche, the somatic scientist seeks to understand the psyche in terms of human bodily behavior. From the somatic viewpoint, study of the living, functioning body *is* the study of the psyche. It is a viewpoint that stands psychology on its head, becoming—in a word—somatology.

The comparative study of bodily behavior achieved worldwide attention when the two great ethologists Konrad Lorenz and Nikko Tinbergen received a Nobel prize. Ethologists study animal behavior from a somatic viewpoint: They understand that what we call "behavior" is, after all, a series of movement patterns in time. Different species of animals typically have species-specific patterns of behavior. A specific sequence of movement patterns is typical of the mating behavior of a graylag goose, or the hunting behavior of a lion or the parental bonding of a just-hatched mallard duck. Phylogenetically— that is, by genetic inheritance—each species has its own typical patterns of behavior that are so "fixed" in the species that they define that particular species. We are able to make a specific identification of a racoon, for example, by describing its physical characteristics—its bodily structure; but without any knowledge of the bodily structure of a racoon, we can identify its species with equal exactness by describing its typical ways of behaving—its functional patterns.

This attention to bodily functions is not new. Indeed, it is a knowledge that is as old as the earliest human hunters, who knew precisely how their animal prey moved, fled, hid and fought. The earliest human lore about animals characterized the ways in which animals thought: The bestiary fables of primitive humans deduced what was typically in the "minds" of monkeys, tigers and elephants from the typical ways in which they "behaved," i.e., moved their bodies. The animal lore of primitive societies is somatic. But what is new about this, since Darwin and his seminal *Expressions of the Emotions in Man and Animals,* is the controlled scientific observation, measurement and cataloging of different species of behavior. With ethology, the science of species-specific functions was born, and it has transformed our understanding of the entire animal kingdom, including ourselves.

Nowhere is this transformation more significant than in its import for understanding the nature of the human being. A functional description of the human being is momentous for one very special reason: It allows us to understand *the optimal state of human functioning.* In a word, it gives us, for the first time, a scientific basis for determining what is human health. Those functional patterns that are phylogenetically typical of human behavior are, by definition, those evolved patterns of human action that are the most efficient for enhancing the survival of the human individual. If we know how the human is phylogenetically *designed* to function, we then know how the human *qua* human functions best. If some of these typical functions are lacking, then we automatically know that the human is functioning less than fully, less than is necessary for his best chances at survival. Because it focuses on function, the somatic viewpoint offers us a nascent science, capable not only of describing the specific nature of human beings but also, simultaneously, the optimal state of health that is specifically human.

It must be immediately pointed out that a somatic science of *Homo sapiens* is to be sharply distinguished from the speculations of neo-Darwinians. Such writers as Robert Ardrey and Desmond Morris, and a host of others, have alleged certain fixed patterns in human behavior which control and motivate human behavior in a deterministic fashion, whether this be territorial defense or aggressive hunting behavior. Such speculations fly in the face of the enormous variety and unpredictability of human behavior—one of the fundamental traits of the human individual, amply documented anthropologically not only in the prodigious varieties of human cultures but also, more importantly, in the countless exceptions to any one of these cultures by the individuals within them. The speculations of the neo-Darwinians are clear examples of an inability to think somatically, of the failure to stand psychology on its head. Indeed, such views are blatant examples of the positivism that has haunted scientific psychology from the beginning: the allegation that humans are determined, rather than free; that they are ultimately predictable, rather than ultimately unpredictable.

In categorical contrast to any attempt to portray humans as subhuman, somatic thinkers and scientists describe the typical human in ways that are distinctly nonpsychological. These are ways that, at first, seem subtle and unimportant: such things as the balance of the human biped over gravity, the efficient coordination of human movement, the posture of the living body, the ability of the human to express its needs (*whatever* they may be), the ability of a human to experience an orderly external world (*whatever* it may appear to be). These are factors of direct importance to the ability of the human to function adequately in the ecological and physical world. Per se, these are not psychological factors; they are somatic factors, namely, underlying ways in which the human bodily structure must function in the worldly environment.

Somatic factors are invariant functions—functions that affect the efficiency and survival of all human individuals, however great their differences. They point to nonpsychological events that are far more substantive than the "psychological" behavior learned through the verbal human culture. And because they are invariant factors, we can make valid judgments, both within ourselves and in others, as to whether the underpinnings of efficient, survival-enhancing human behavior are present.

If we know what are certain invariant functions in the human creature, and if we know that the full presence of these functions guarantees a fully human way of functioning, then we have in our possession a knowledge that is simultaneously a way of behaving—a *gnosis* that is also a *praxis*. This is what is new about the somatic point of view: For the first time it permits us to establish a norm for human life and behavior. There *is* a nature common to humans and specific to our species. Until recently we simply did not know how and where to look for it: in the body of functions typical of all human beings.

The visionary scientists and thinkers who have developed the somatic view of humankind offer us much more than a picture of the healthy, optimally functioning human; by the very nature of their concern, their vision is a healing vision— a vision that points the way toward health. The somatic vision is a healing vision of the most composite kind: It points simultaneously toward the healing of mind, the healing of body and the healing of society. From the somatic viewpoint, the three are inseparable. They are bound together in a single conception of the nature of the human being, and it is this understanding of human nature that provides the theme of this book.

The somatic vision of human nature can be developed from a variety of scientific viewpoints: from that of physics and cybernetics (Moshe Feldenkrais), psychoanalysis (Alexander Lowen), biochemistry (Ida Rolf), proprioception (Charlotte Selver and Charles Brooks), psychophysiology (Barbara Brown), physical anthropology (Ashley Montagu), neuropsychology (Karl Pribram), psychotherapy (Carl Rogers) and cultural anthropology (Margaret Mead). From all of these varied standpoints the somatic vision is the common denominator: The focus is on the embodied functions of living, adapting human beings.

Any viewpoint capable of giving a common direction to so many scientific perspectives is not, you may suspect, simplistic: It is a complex of a number of assumptions which have gradually established themselves during the course of this century. So that we can better appreciate the richness of this fascinating perspective, we should now take a brief look at the assumptions that are central to the somatic viewpoint.

SOME BASIC ASSUMPTIONS OF THE SOMATIC VIEWPOINT

1. *Life is historical.* The somatic viewpoint sees the human being—and all living beings—within a historical perspective. This is to say that humans are viewed transparently in terms of the layers of genetic history that are reflected in the struc-

ture and functions of *Homo sapiens.* Viewed in evolutionary transparency, this hand is, by historical extension, a fin, or this ear is a gill slit, or this lateral movement of the infant's body is the lateral flexion of a fish's undulation.

It is in examining the historicity of human structure and function that we begin to understand the how and the why of the human creature—the how of a man's sneer (the threatening display of the canine teeth) or the why of a woman's menses (the lunar cycles of beings who first procreated in the sea). Such human traits are incomprehensible if the human being is studied only at the superficial layer of his presently evolved appearance. The somatic perspective knows that the human can be seen roundly and wholly only if seen deeply in terms of his historical lineage, a lineage which, ultimately, leads us backward to the earliest life forms and those earthly conditions which made that formation possible.

2. *All life is individual.* In its classifications and in its theorizing, biology may use general abstractions, such as animal "kingdom" and "species" and gene "pools," but in simple fact all of life has only one essential form: that of the individual—the single soma. Somatic scientists do not allow the usefulness of general abstractions to obscure the fact that the phenomenon of life assembles itself within single packages. Life must form itself into the unified structure of a cell; whether it be a single-celled animal or a higher-order protozoan animal assembling millions of cells, the identifiable animal is a unified body of functions enclosed within a single membrane.

This recognition of the systematic integrity of the soma is, at the human level, *a recognition of the person.* The ultimate reality of *Homo sapiens* is not the race and is not the culture. The ultimate human reality is *the self.* From the somatic point of view, any inability to recognize selfhood as the essential reality of humanness is a failure to understand both human life and life in general. Equally, failure to recognize the uniqueness of the human self is considered to be ultimately harmful to individuals.

This is to say that somatic thought always sees abstract generalizations—whether manufactured by science or by the political state—as the enemy of humankind. Humankind is always individuated into unique selves, and any scientific theory or political practice that ignores this individuality is unhealthy for humans *qua* humans.

Put positively, the optimal possibilities for healing and continuing health occur when each human is treated as a special case. For men such as Rogers and Feldenkrais, to do otherwise would be a travesty of the nature of therapy and human growth.

3. *Individual life is autonomous.* Implicit in twentieth-century biology is the assumption that living, individual creatures —namely, somas—are self-governing. Somas of every species have emerged and survived because they are, at every moment in their lives, adaptive. Adaptation of the individual creature to the environment (accommodation) and adaptation of the environment to the individual creature (assimilation) is a constant feature of somatic functioning.

In the human species this self-balancing and self-adjusting ability has immediate application to the ways humans are educated, healed and socialized. The somatic attitude in education is, quite simply, that humans must become self-educating. In therapy, the attitude is that humans must be allowed to be self-healing. In social structures, the attitude is that the most efficient society is one that assumes internal adjustment of individuals, one to another. In all three instances, the understanding is that authentic and optimal human education, therapy and society do not require the external imposition of force or control.

This recognition of the self-regulating autonomy of human life shows the somatic attitude to be radically democratic in that *it assumes individual responsibility to be a biological fact.* As a factual capacity that is genetically given to all humans, this responsibility for one's learned abilities, for one's health and growth, as well as for one's position in society, predicates a biological basis for a free human society. According to this view, there is a phylogenetic basis to Jefferson's claim that all humans are free and possess inalienable rights.

This is a somatic theme that is either expressed or implied in all of the essays which follow. The constant self-adjustment occurring in the biofeedback phenomenon is basic to Barbara Brown's insight into the seemingly unlimited capacities of the human. The self-adjusting nature of human neural functions is implicit in Karl Pribram's holographic theory of human perception and memory. Likewise, it would be impossible to appreciate the thinking of Margaret Mead without understanding that individual responsibility is at the core of her thinking. Finally, Carl Rogers's famous conception of "client-centered" therapy assumes that the human individual must be encouraged to be self-regulating and responsible.

4. *Individuals are temporal beings in process.* All life manifests itself in somas—i.e., individual bodies of functions—and these bodies are always in process. The recognition that living beings are temporal beings is essential to the somatic vision, and it is a corrective to the traditional temptation to think of somas in static terms—namely, as things.

In all scientific observation of life, the living process must be stopped in order to be studied; otherwise, no measurement is possible. Living beings are laid out on a dissecting table for the purpose of static observation. Or they are observed through the stop-action frames of films or stroboscopes. Or they are assumed to have constant and invariable functions. Observing a living subject as static is an inescapable feature of scientific research, and because of its inescapability, scientists can be easily lulled into the error of conceiving of living organisms as things that are stationary in space.

Human science is, like human language, a spatializing, fixating operation, leading to the formulation of principles and laws which, on the surface, appear static. But the somatic attitude is a constant reminder that life, because it is constantly in motion, is essentially temporal in nature and cannot be theoretically reduced to a spatial "thing" without falsifying the nature of life.

Somas are either living or they are dead, and in the latter case they are no longer somas, but have reverted back to the inert things of which the life process is biophysically constituted. Somatic thinking is of one mind with such twentieth-century philosophers as Bergson, Whitehead and Heidegger in seeing the essential nature of the human as temporal and the central substance of life as a continuing, integrated process whose motion is temporally forward. Living beings—human or otherwise—are not, finally, "in time"; instead, they are processes that continuously *create* the fact of temporality, always moving, always flowing, always adapting until the moment of death, when the process ceases and the individual life is no more.

One of the paradoxes of human life is that humans yearn and

strive for finality and completion—i.e., for a static state—
constantly forgetting that such a state is impossible. Finality is
always just beyond human achievement and is antipathetic to
life: At the moment of achieving it, life is no longer life.
Charlotte Selver and Charles Brooks have, throughout their
careers, been engrossed with the process of life; their concern
is to develop the ability of experiencing this ongoing process
as it occurs within oneself. This absorption of human awareness
within the immediacy of one's life process is, as was earlier
expressed, a *praxis* as well as a *gnosis:* a practical healing, as
well as a knowing, can thereby take place. In a similar fashion,
Ashley Montagu—a man devoted to "growing young"—sees
the human task of managing one's own process and enhancing
it as one of life's great invitations.

5. *Life is predominantly functional rather than structural.*
This theme is an extension of the understanding of life as,
essentially, a process. But what is specifically implied by this
recognition of functional dominance is a theme that has already been touched upon: namely, the need to see through
bodily structure in order to determine the functions motivating
that structure.

Somatic thinking transcends the traditional dichotomy of
the human being into "mind" and "body," establishing a view
more in accordance with the nature of biological process: the
distinction between structure and function. In living creatures
the "bodily" structure, being a temporal process, is something
far less substantial than a spatial object. Human structure is
soft, permeable, ephemeral and insubstantial; it is not a body
in the way that an inert physical object is a body. In fact, to
think of living beings primarily in such physical terms is a
deception. An organism may look like a physical object, but

that is an illusion. Beneath the flowing contours of the bodily process are stable functions, represented in the central nervous system, which create this illusion of physical substantiality. This is not to say that human functions are independent of bodily structure, but rather that they have a primacy in the process of human life. Here is the way Barbara Brown expresses this typical theme: "Mind is an energy of brain capable of functioning independently of brain, although born of it and sustained by the physical activity of it."

What is uncanny is that the "body" of a human being is not a physical body so much as it is a system of constant functions. Without these functions there would be no "body" at all. This theme of functional *order* is fundamental in the essays of both Feldenkrais and Pribram. In a broader fashion, the assumption of functional dominance is central to the thinking and therapy of Alexander Lowen, who sees energetic functioning to be the vibrant core of bodily process. Most strikingly, this is also the view of Ida Rolf in her practice of "structural" integration, which modifies human structure so that there is a reduction of entropy in human functioning.

6. *Self-consciousness is body-consciousness.* Somatic think-ers are not encumbered by the clumsy schism of human beings into minds and bodies: Humans are both, at the same time and as part of the same process. This is nowhere more apparent than in the human experience of self-awareness. From the somatic point of view, self-awareness *is* body-awareness—it is awareness of the ongoing, stable process of our bodily structure. What other "self" is there to be aware of, other than our embodied self?

Self-awareness is a central preoccupation of Lowen, Fel-denkrais, Selver, Brooks and Brown, all of whom understand (along with the entire phenomenological tradition) that consciousness is always "consciousness *of*"—specifically, consciousness of one's bodily process.

7. *All living beings seek to grow.* This observation is in the background of all somatic thinking and healing, and is responsible for the hopeful and positive attitude characterizing all somatic thought. This theme can be viewed *en large* in terms of the total history of evolved life, or it can be focused on the growth of individuals. In either, the observation is the same: Life seeks to differentiate itself into newness and greater complexity.

Perhaps the clearest image for the nature of growth is the image of the tree: Rooted in the world, it surges upward as a main trunk, then differentiates into limbs, then further branches out into twigs, which grow and once again differentiate into ever greater complexity.

In reading these essays on the nature of human life, one can sense this image of the tree of life standing behind all of these richly varied scientific viewpoints. The healing vision is a vision of life as growing, a process of branching out into richer complexity, differentiation and newness. From the somatic point of view, life becomes more whole by growing into greater difference: Growth is healing and healing is growth. The growing edge of life is always different, always *new*. Quite simply, without life there would be nothing new: Newness is life's most precious creation.

THOMAS HANNA

MOSHE FELDENKRAIS

The English of Queen Elizabeth's time distinguished the "quick" from the "dead." "Quick" was a word meaning "living," and it meant this in the specific sense of "that which moves."

The double meaning of the word quick is as characteristic of the thinking of Moshe Feldenkrais as it is of sixteenth-century English: For both, the living is that which moves, and the dead is that which does not. For this physicist-turned-healer, the prime characteristic of life is movement, and by extension, the more movement there is, the more life there is.

Born in eastern Russia in 1904, Feldenkrais emigrated to Israel while still in his teens. As a young man in Israel, he became successful as a special tutor, teaching learning-disabled students the ability to learn. "Learning how to learn" became a lifelong educational concern of Feldenkrais's. As a teacher, he was less concerned with the content of learning than with the learning process itself.

In Paris he earned his doctorate in electrical engineering, specializing in high-energy physics. Shortly afterward he began a long research association with Nobel laureate, Frédéric Joliot-Curie, in the famous Radium Laboratories founded by Madame Curie. Feldenkrais's scientific work during the 1930s was focused on nuclear fission. But, characteristically, he was equally proficient in judo—becoming

Europe's first holder of the black belt—and in soccer. It was a severe knee injury, incurred in the latter sport, that eventually led Feldenkrais to an intense study of anatomy, physiology, psychology and anthropology, all in a successful effort to heal a knee that showed little chance of being repaired through surgery.

When the Nazi army entered France, Feldenkrais fled to England, where he was a scientific officer of the British Admiralty, working on antisubmarine warfare. After the war he returned to Israel where, from 1949 to 1952, he was director of electronics research for Israel's Ministry of Defense. Feldenkrais had already begun to practice his technique of neuromuscular education, called Functional Integration. After 1952 he devoted himself full time to the practice of Functional Integration at his famous institute on Nachmani Street in Tel Aviv.

As early as 1929 Dr. Feldenkrais published his first book on judo and throughout the 1930s published a series of volumes on judo, both in French and in English, which explored the bodily mechanics and theory of judo combat. It was this analysis of the dynamics of efficient bodily movement which, in combination with his increasing awareness of the cybernetic nature of the central nervous system, led to the formulation of Functional Integration.

As he describes it, Functional Integration takes place "in the lying position, prone or supine, to facilitate the breaking down of muscular patterns. The habitual pressures on the soles of the feet and the ensuing configuration of the skeletal joints are suppressed. The nervous system does not receive the habitual afferent stimuli due to gravitation, and the efferent impulses are not linked into habitual patterns. After the lessons, on receiving again the habitual stimuli, one is surprised to discover a changed response to them."

These changed responses occur in victims of severely crippling diseases, such as cerebral palsy, multiple sclerosis, and polio, as well as spastic paralysis due to traumatic injury. The same techniques are said to be equally successful in training athletes, musicians and actors in improving the efficiency of their movements. Thus, Functional Integration, as a technique for bodily education, has both clinical and educational applications.

Up until the 1970s only thirteen persons had been trained to practice Functional Integration, but in 1975 Feldenkrais accepted this editor's invitation to establish a three-year training program in San Francisco for some sixty-five students. With the completion of that program, The Feldenkrais Guild was formed, representing the more than seventy-five persons in North America and Europe capable of doing Functional Integration. These same persons also teach Awareness Through Movement, the name given by Feldenkrais to his system of group exercises, which are extensions of the working principles of Functional Integration.

It is important to note that Feldenkrais has devised an educational system—not a therapeutic system. He is concerned to improve functions, rather than correct them. This should be remembered when contrasting Functional Integration with Alexander Lowen's Bioenergetics or Ida Rolf's Structural Integration, both of which are not only in the tradition of medical therapy but also aim to have psychological-emotional benefits, rather than simply physical benefits. According to Feldenkrais, there are indeed psychological benefits from Functional Integration, but they are seen as the inevitable effect of the overall improvements in efficient functioning which occur when neural functions are better integrated.

BIBLIOGRAPHY

1_____.La defénse du faible contre l'agresseur 1932.
2_____.ABC de judo 1937.
3_____.Higher Judo. 3 vols. 1942
4_____.Judo. 1942
5_____.Body and Mature Behavior 1949.
6_____.Awareness Through Movement. 1972.
7_____.The Case of Nora. 1977.

Man and the World

MOSHE FELDENKRAIS

CONSISTING of an astronomical number of cells, the human nervous system is fit to live and function in a great variety of physical worlds. As the experience of so many astronauts has shown, our nervous system can stand up to a lack of gravitation and to the practical absence of both auditory and visual stimulation. In order to maintain awareness at its normal level, it was enough for the astronauts to initiate activities in which a sufficient number of successive cues occurred at close intervals.

I believe that our nervous system would function well in a thousand different possible worlds. It would grow and adapt itself, or better still, it would learn to act and respond to any conditions in which life can exist. Because it seeks order and consistency, our nervous system can, for example, be "wired in" to cope easily with any of the three thousand languages, and as many dialects, that exist on earth.

The cosmos (meaning "order" in Greek) is not very predictable, except for a few things like day and night, lunar phases and the seasons. I am not sure that simpler nervous systems are aware even of these orderly phenomena. Otherwise, randomness is the rule. Meteorites have a very disorderly way of falling.

No one can predict which atom will disintegrate at a given moment in any radioactive material. The falling of a particular raindrop at a precise place and instant is anybody's guess. The situation is the same with earthquakes, winds, typhoons, suns and galaxies, as well as on the microscopic level with solids, gasses or liquids. Whatever we may choose for examination, there is little that is predictable, orderly, stable and invariant. In most phenomena too many parameters are involved to detect cause and effect, which to us means order.

But nervous structures look for order and will find it when and where it can be found or can be asserted. Only nervous systems, consisting of such great numbers of units as there are in most living creatures, need consistency and constancy of environment. To form a self, to find a mate, to live in a herd, flock or society, it is imperative to have an organization that is repetitive so that it will be possible to learn to cope with the world. For the more complex life forms—monkeys swinging from one branch to another thirty feet away or humans playing tennis or violins—it is essential for them to form sets of invariants which allow learning while growing. This is a type of learning quite apart from academic learning.

When born, all living creatures are smaller and weaker than their grown-up parents, some for shorter and some for longer intervals of time. Weak organisms need a consistent and constant world in order to grow into strong adults. As we know, an organism is within itself an entire world of micro-beings which needs, in its turn, a consistent outside world so that the internal world can have homeostasis, order and invariance—a condition that must be maintained if it is to exist at all for any length of time.

In short, a living nervous system introduces order into the

random, constantly changing stimuli arriving through the senses and impinging on the system. Moreover, the living organism itself is moving incessantly, and the nervous system has to bring order to the mobile, changing world, as well as to its own mobility, to make some sense from this whirling turmoil.

Quite surprisingly, the most efficient means for achieving this herculean feat is *movement. Movement* of the living organism is essential for the formation of *stationary* events in the changing, moving environment and the constantly moving organism itself. Even if we are observing inert matter, our senses still perceive moving impressions, since a living organism is never completely stationary until it dies.

Professor Heinz Von Foerster, a cyberneticist who nourishes similar ideas, has noted that the French mathematician Henri Poincaré wrote in 1887 that three-dimensional vision is possible not only because there are two eyes, but also because of the movement of the head which carries them. The head movements need the adjustment of the eyes, and three-dimensional pictures would not be perceived with eyes that were merely stationary in space.

Von Foerster has also told of a Swiss ski instructor, a man named Kohler, who persuaded some of his pupils to participate in a fascinating experiment. He wanted to find out what would happen if our brain saw the outside world as it is on the retina, and not as it actually is. As everyone knows, the eye lens, like any other lens, inverts the image on the retina. When seen, a standing person has his head at the bottom of the retina and his feet at the top. Kohler gave all the participants a pair of glasses inverting the image on the retina to be the right way up. As expected, he and all the others saw everything upside down. The first hours were very difficult; nobody could move freely or do anything without going very slowly and trying to figure out and make sense of what he or she saw. Then something unexpected happened: Everything about their bodies and the immediate vicinity that they were touching began to look as before, but everything which could not be touched continued to be inverted. Gradually, by groping and touching while moving around to attain the satisfaction of normal needs, participants in the experiment found that objects further afield began to appear normal to the participants in the experiment. In a few weeks, everything looked the right way up, and they could all do everything without any special attention or care. At one point in the experiment snow began to fall. Kohler looked through the window and saw the flakes rising from the earth and moving upwards. He went out, stretched out his hands, palms upwards, and felt the snow falling on them. After only a few moments of feeling the snow touch his palms, he began to see the snow falling instead of rising.

There have been other experiments with inverted spectacles. One carried out in the United States involved two people, one sitting in a wheelchair and the other pushing it, both fitted with such special glasses. The one who moved around by pushing the chair began to see normally and, after a few hours, was able to find his way without groping, while the one sitting continued to see everything the wrong way.

Does a newborn baby see the right way from the start? Or does the infant instead, have to move and touch things in order to be able to interpret and give order to the impressions he receives? I, for one, suspect that movement plays a central role in forming our objective world. And, if my suspicion is not altogether wrong, movement may be necessary for all living things to form their orderly, objective, exterior world, and perhaps even their internal image of the world.

One thing is certain: We are not merely the realization of the program of our given genetic code. We know that the realization of this program never happens without the growth of the organism bearing that genetic code. Moreover, being born and growing never happens without at least one observer or witness—the one that gives birth to the new organism. And, in addition, no living organism is known to exist outside a gravitational field.

In sum, a genetic program is incorporated into a body that grows from two cells to whatever number of cells, in an environment inevitably situated in a gravitational field that is never without witnesses. None of these items—the genetic code, the witnesses, the gravitational field—can alone, by any stretch of the imagination, form a living being able to grow and become adult.

All mammals have skeletons, muscles and nervous systems, and they are born to parents, and the earth exercises on all of them the same gravitational force that is never interrupted and cannot be screened. Man, being a mammal, shares this estate. There are, however, important differences. The human skeleton has the thumbs so structured that he can touch the tips of all of his fingers. An orangutan or chimpanzee has in its arms power-producing muscles stronger than man's, but the fine musculature of the human hand allows for a manipulative range of extreme finesse. Think of writing, making music, watchmaking, etc. The functional differences of the nervous system of man set him apart from all other mammals. Parenthood in man is also very different. A human child usually has a father and a mother, plus two grandfathers and two grand-

24   *Moshe Feldenkrais*

mothers. The human environment involves the self and the self-image, as well as the sexual, the social and cultural, besides the spatial and temporal aspects of it.

The movements involved in every action produce a displacement of the entire organism with changes in its configuration, all of which affect different aspects of the environment, in order to provide for the necessities of the organism. There is, then, a continuously changing environment with a continuously changing organism, both interacting without cease so long as there is life in the organism. Different environments affect the organism and the nervous system so as to cause it to act and react effectively and efficiently to these changes.

We have then, from birth till death, a closed loop of four elements: skeleton, muscles, nervous system and environment. These elements are, in fact, very complex systems interacting with numerous feedbacks and feedforwards all along the loop. The loop can be drawn as a quadrangle with four sides and four summits. In my own work I deal mostly with the summits rather than with the sides. I deal with the linkage at the summits, where the elements interact with one another and where the learned use of self is more apparent. The individual life of intentional activity and reacting can more easily be changed through learning than through the more rigid structures represented by the sides, i.e., bones, muscles, nervous system and space-culture-time-etc. It is also better to improve the *way* we do things than *what* we do. For *how* we do something is of more importance than what we do.

These four complex elements can be studied from the beginning of life to the end. At birth the organism-environmental link is largely passive. By and by, passivity is replaced by more and more intentional activity. Were there no gravitation, the whole scheme would be radically different. Bones would not be built to withstand compression. Velocity and power of movements would be different. It would be something that we could hardly conceive. As it is, *movement is the best clue to life.* Ever since man has been able to speak, he has classified all existing things according to their movement in the gravitational field. Vegetation is everything which moves passively from side to side, following the flow of water or air; otherwise, its growth is vertical. Living things are classified after the way they move. The swimming ones are fishes, the flying ones are birds, the gliding ones are snakes, the wriggling ones are worms. There are jumping ones, crawling ones, the ones that walk on all fours and we, featherless bipeds, who walk upright. Movement seems to have preoccupied man since he could first remember himself.

Movement is central to each living cell making up the organism, and the whole of it—the skeleton, the muscles and the nervous system—is preoccupied with movement. The organization of movement is so complex that most living things need some personal, individual apprenticeship, be they fishes, birds, apes or men. The amount of apprenticeship varies from a few seconds or minutes to many years. Some of the herd animals —especially the bovines, horses, zebras, and their like—seem to be able to follow the herd almost immediately after they are dropped by the mother cow, mare, or whatever. The newborn will make an attempt or two to get on its feet immediately after its umbilical cord is chewed and it is licked all over. When the second or third attempt at standing is successful, the calf will follow the cow on sand, gravel or slippery wet grass, no matter whether it is on level, ascending or descending ground. It can not only do everything necessary to cling to the herd, but it also can right itself if it happens to slide or stumble. If one thinks of the complexity and ingenuity necessary to construct a machine which is similarly efficient, one can realize what is involved in this extraordinary ability to move without previous experience and with so little apprenticeship.

Think of the mountain goats, whose kids are born on high rocks. The kids right themselves and then have to leap from one sharp edge to another without previous apprenticeship. Obviously, all the connections, the "wiring-in" of the nervous systems of these animals, must be made before they are born. In short, with nonhuman animals it is the species which has handed down the learning, the evolving, the reflex organization, the instinct which enables them to survive in precarious conditions. However, most birds, dogs, kittens of all sorts (even tiger kittens), have to have some kind of coaching by their parents to finish the wiring-in, establishing the functioning patterns of their nervous systems. That which can make this pattern reliable, autonomous or automatic needs an apprenticeship of a few weeks.

When we pass in review many of the species, it becomes evident that the *lower* a species's place on the ladder of evolution, the more complete is the wiring-in of the nervous system at birth. The connections of the synapses, neurons and whatever are ready, and the apprenticeship is shorter, the lower the species are on the ladder. In man, we see the extreme end of this process. The human infant has, to my knowledge, the longest apprenticeship of all the species. Although everything necessary to maintain life and growth is already connected in the nervous and glandular systems at birth, the specific human functions are not wired in at all. No baby was every born who could speak, sing, whistle, crawl, walk upright, make music, count, think mathematically or tell the hour of the day or night. Without a very long apprenticeship, lasting several years, none of these functions has ever been observed to develop. As far as these specifically human functions or activities go, the connections, or the wiring-in, of the neural structures are nonexistent at birth.

It is the individual, personal experience, or apprenticeship, that is necessary, and without it the baby will not be a human being. It is as if there were no inherited learning whatsoever in the human species. The "lower" animals have phylogenetic learning—the inherited and evolved learning of their species. The "higher" animal learns through its own individual ontogenetic experience. The "lower" and "higher" have little meaning other than to refer to the complexity of our way of putting together the ladder of evolution. Almost all the lower animals can do things that the highest can never do without prolonged learning, and then only through imitation, usually with a great variety of auxiliary instruments or structures.

The tendency to repetition leads, in the end, to repetitive constancy and order. Most happenings are ruled by chance and are so disorderly that most goings-on are not predictable. We make the laws of nature by singling out the parts of events to which we can add what we consider order. Newton made order in an impressive array of disorderly falling bodies by promoting gravitation to the status of being.

Only nervous tissues and systems are capable of conceiving and realizing. In human beings it is the neural substance that organizes order in its own functioning; it makes order in its environment, which in turn improves the orderliness of the human, and so on. The neural substance organizes itself and thereby selects and alters the incoming messages from the environment into invariant sets, thus making repetition possible. Many continuously changing messages are received from the environment before the organism succeeds in perceiving them as unchanging entities. So great is the ability of the nervous system that it creates order where instruments made of any other matter will register a blur of continuous variations. Just think of taking a photograph of a greyhound running towards you while you are sitting on a galloping horse. We can understand each other while a fan or an air conditioner makes so much background noise that no recorder will reproduce an intelligible record of what we said. We have no difficulty extracting invariant order out of many varying interferences. In anything we see, hear, smell or feel, we actively organize ourselves so as to be impressed by those invariant sets that allow us to cope with the disorder both within ourselves and outside ourselves in the environment, whether interpersonal, social, spatial or temporal.

Put simply: A thing is alive if it has a boundary separating it from the rest of the world, if it can reproduce itself, if it can maintain itself (i.e., draw energy from outside its boundary), and if it can preserve itself. All these functions cannot occur without self-direction, i.e., movement. The widening of awareness through movement is a learning process that has been used ever since the first cell took on a membrane and became an individual needing to direct itself.

Awareness Through Movement is a learning process that makes self-direction easier and more pleasurable, because it resembles the learning that occurs with growth itself. The two methods I use, Awareness Through Movement and Functional Integration are essentially an efficient, short and general way of *learning to learn.* In traditional learning it is *what* we learn that is important. But the higher function of learning to learn is free of such restrictions. Learning to learn involves an improvement of the brain function itself, which carries it beyond its latent potential.

To facilitate such learning it is necessary to divorce the aim to be achieved from the learning process itself. The process is the important thing and should be aimless to the adult learner just as is learning to the baby. The baby is not held to any timetable, nor is there any need to rely on force. Reeducation of the adult has been corrupted by the teaching methods traditionally learned in schools and by academic teaching in general. In both, the teacher is presumed to be superior to the learner and is an example to follow and to imitate. Achievement is the aim, not learning; and precise times are fixed for specific achievements. Learning such as this has nothing to do with growth: It can be delayed at will or even abandoned altogether. But the learning that is dependent on growth cannot be delayed with impunity, nor can it be accelerated beyond the normal pace of growth.

I believe that the possibility of a better future humanity is nearer to our grasp than is presumed by the gloomy outlook of self-destruction that is predicted and held by many. A society in which its members are only so many units composing it is not the final form of society. A society of men and women with greater awareness of themselves will, I believe, be one that will work for the human dignity of its members rather than primarily for the abstract, collective notion of human society.

ALEXANDER LOWEN

The life of Dr. Alexander Lowen has spanned two careers and two professions. In 1934 he was admitted to the practice of law in New York State. In 1953 he was admitted to the practice of medicine in New York State. Between those two dates he studied for twelve years with one of the major figures of modern psychotherapy, Wilhelm Reich. From that twelve-year association came the construction of a therapeutic system which Dr. Lowen named Bioenergetics and which has obtained worldwide fame.

Alexander Lowen has the uncanny ability of seeing an individual's personality by looking at that person's body. For him, to look closely at the human body is to look closely at the human heart, whose vibrant force animates that body. Bioenergetics is the way Dr. Lowen has devised to free that heart from the tyranny of a disordered body.

Lowen was a practicing attorney when he met Wilhelm Reich in 1940. Reich was the most passionate of the students of Sigmund Freud. Those passions carried him to affirm so strongly the sexual and orgastic implications of Freud's thinking that he became a renegade within the psychoanalytic tradition.

Reich, like all psychoanalysts, saw therapeutic healing as that which occurred when the suppressed information of the unconscious was made conscious. This event is catharsis. What Reich saw—and what no other psychoanalyst saw—was that the agency for the repression of psychic information was the body itself: namely, the musculature. The jaw muscles will take on unconscious rigidity in holding back the anger and biting behavior felt by the patient. The shoulders are bound in the effort to keep from striking. The orbicular muscles around the eyes remain frozen in constant and unrelieved fear in the face of the ever wide-eyed girl who suffered an anxious childhood. Muscles in the perineum and the pelvis prevent the movement and circulation that would allow a full and free orgasm.

What Reich did was to somaticize the concepts of repression and the unconscious: He took them out of the vacuous realm of psychology and saw them as physiological functions—muscles frozen in stasis so as not to express the forbidden emotions the patient really needs to express. Reich was not opposed to the traditional verbal therapy, he simply believed that until the musculature of the body was rendered more supple and expressive, there was no possibility for verbal therapy to have success.

But the radical emphasis of Reich was upon what he called "orgastic potency." He saw human orgasm as an innate reflex action which, after building up a larger and larger charge, culminated by releasing that charge in the convulsions of orgasm. The greater the orgasm, the greater the release of pent-up tension. Hence, one of the prime aims of therapy was to free the patient from the somatic repressions of his or her orgastic potency. Reich also suggested that without orgastic potency, the psychoanalyst himself was defective as both man and analyst. This later point of contention hastened his expulsion from the Psychoanalytic Association.

Alexander Lowen first met Reich when the latter was teaching a course on psychoanalysis at the New School for Social Research. The two became friends, and eventually Lowen decided to go through psychoanalysis with Reich, only to discover that Reich wanted him not to talk, but to breath. This first session allowed Lowen to discover the "muscular armoring" in his own chest to relive a repressed scene not remembered since his infanthood. As Lowen's work with Reich developed, he realized that a medical degree would be necessary if he were to establish his work as a psychoanalyst.

Although Reich worked directly with the body, using deep muscular massage on such places as the pelvis and jaw, his attention to the body was far less than Lowen felt was needed. In developing Bioenergetics, Lowen diverged from Reich's vegeto-therapy in two respects: He felt that Reich failed to exploit the full movement and expressive potential of the body—a more active, bodily therapy was needed; secondly, he felt that Reich failed to complete and reinforce the psychoanalytic process because he did not make a thorough verbal analysis of the information generated by bodily catharsis.

One of the prime characteristics of Bioenergetics is the large number of exercises developed by Lowen, exercises designed to excite bodily catharsis and release, through vigorous experiences of sobbing, screaming or pounding fists and feet in a childlike tantrum. These, as well as less traumatic exercises, are all designed to unblock the repression of libidinal energy, allowing that energy to vibrate and flow in a healthy fashion throughout the entire body. In his own bodily life, Alexander Lowen is a glowing exemplar of the vibrant health and *joie de vivre* to which he invites his patients.

BIBLIOGRAPHY

1_____. *The Physical Dynamics of Character Structure,* 1958.
2_____.*Love and Orgasm,* 1965.
3_____.*Betrayal of the Body,* 1967.
4_____.*Pleasure,* 1970.
5_____.*Depression and the Body,* 1972.
6_____.*Bioenergetics,* 1975.
7_____. *The Way to Vibrant Health: A Manual of Bioenergetic Exercises,* 1977.

Human Nature

ALEXANDER LOWEN

I WOULD like to pay homage to my teacher, Wilhelm Reich, who belongs in the fore ranks of those who have explored the nature of humankind. His contributions to our understanding of life and nature are among the greatest. Reich was the first person to understand the complex relationship of mind and body. In contrast to those who saw mind and body as distinct entities and to those who claimed they were one, Reich formulated the concept of psychosomatic unity and antithesis. He showed that the bodily attitude (somatic expression) was functionally identical with the mental attitude (psychic expression). Both were aspects of the character structure. At the same time mind and body influence each other. On the superficial level they are reciprocal: Thinking affects the body just as bodily events influence thinking.

Reich started as a psychoanalyst, a member of Freud's circle. His first contribution was the concept of character analysis, which has long been regarded as one of the major advances in psychoanalytic thinking. According to this concept, a patient's present-day mode of behavior is to be analyzed before material from the past, early childhood, is to be given much credence. Fritz Perls, who had been analyzed by Reich as I was, made the concept of character analysis the basis of gestalt therapy in terms of an emphasis upon the here and now of a patient's behavior.

Reich's next great contribution was the concept of armoring. The armor is a set of muscular tensions which serve to protect the person both from outer attack and from his own impulses. The armor is part of the character structure which defines an individual's fixed pattern of behavior. If we know the character structure of an individual, we can predict how he will react. Generally the character structure is determined by the age of six to eight years. It is formed as a result of the experiences that the child goes through in growing up. These experiences are registered not only in the mind but also in the body. They shape the body by structuring the permissible responses to life situations. Responses which are not allowed expression are inhibited or blocked by chronic muscular tensions. For example, if parents threaten a child for crying or screaming, chronic tensions develop in the throat to suppress these impulses. Sucking and biting impulses are suppressed by chronic tensions in the musculature of the jaw. Impulses to reach out or to strike out are blocked by chronic tensions in the shoulder girdle.

Growing up in civilized communities means that the child has to learn to curb his natural responses. He can't bite someone if he is angry. He is not allowed to take a candy bar from the shelf of a supermarket because he wants it and it is within reach. He has to be toilet trained; in effect, he has to be "housebroken" like our pets. I am not saying that this is all bad. Much depends on how this training is done. If it is done with respect for the child's feelings and with affection, it need not be too traumatic. It depends also on how much fulfillment the child is allowed. A child who is deprived of loving contact with his parents and who is subject to severe discipline may end up as a schizophrenic. But a child's personality can also be damaged by being overindulged or overstimulated. Such experiences lead to the development of a psychopathic personality.

Since all experiences are registered in the body, it is possible to read the life history of a person from his body. This is not basically different from what a woodsman does when he reads the life history of a tree from a study of its rings. Those of us who are trained in bioenergetic analysis can see from the form and movement of the body how that individual coped as a child with the stresses of his life situation. The way in which one coped becomes the character of the person, which then sets the pattern for coping with stress in the future. Our character restricts us to certain ways of being, to certain ways of responding. It is a limitation upon our being and upon our freedom; but since it ensured survival as a child, we dare not risk giving it up now.

Character is the way in which we deal with life. If one has a masochistic character structure, for example, one will be handicapped in self-assertion, in expressing opposition or negative feelings. One tends to be submissive to others so as not to lose their affection. People with such character structures have bodies that are heavy, compressed and collapsed due to the holding in of feelings. Our character defines how we handle our feelings and, by extension, how we handle our energy. It determines how much energy we may have.

Society shapes its members to fit into its system. In a highly industrialized society like ours people have to be schooled to fit the very narrow slots on the economic machine. Some are salespeople, others mechanics; some are executives, and others professionals of various kinds. We become so highly specialized that we become like the very machines we serve. It is also true that the machines serve us, but the relationship is reciprocal. We are as much the slaves of our machines as we are their masters. But since the machines will do all the hard work for us, we do not use our bodies, nor do we need much energy. We push buttons which requires little energy.

In fact, a person with energy and life may find it difficult to function satisfactorily in our present system. Could a fully alive person stand for hours punching a register at a checkout counter or collecting quarters in a tollbooth? Of course, such a person could function creatively, but though we talk of creativity, our machine system provides few opportunities for creative expression. Talented people in all creative fields, often have trouble earning a living with their talent. We even discourage too much aliveness in our children. Most parents want their children to be quiet, calm and well behaved, like dolls or puppets. This is especially true of parents who are depressed and cannot tolerate too much activity. In other words, one can survive more assuredly in our culture as a quiet, unaggressive, conforming person than as a vital individual with a mind of his own.

The mechanism through which we depress our energy level is the restriction of respiration. By limiting our oxygen intake we decrease the metabolic activity of the body and reduce our available energy. Very few people in our culture breathe deeply and fully. The breathing of most people, I would say ninety-eight percent, is shallow and limited. It is either diaphragmatic or costal, with very little involvement of the abdomen. Deep abdominal breathing is very rare. Our culture not only forces us to restrict our breathing, but it also pollutes the very air that is essential for our life and well-being. We can only conclude that our culture is, in many respects, life negative and life destructive. It is no wonder that so many people suffer from depression.

Reich was the first to point out the relation between inhibited breathing, a lowered energy level in the organism, and an impoverished emotional life. He didn't say it as directly as that. His focus was upon the modern individual's loss of orgastic potency, which he believed to be the key to understanding neurotic behavior. He recognized that the inhibition of abdominal respiration was the way a child learns to control its sexual feelings. All cultures impose some restrictions upon sexual expression, but Western culture was unique in the degree to which sexuality, especially childhood sexuality, was viewed as sinful and shameful. Character also determines the way the individual copes with his sexual feelings. I have said that it gels about the ages of six to eight because this is the age at which the child finds some resolution to his Oedipal situation.

We must be careful not to delude ourselves into thinking that the current sexual sophistication has eliminated sexual problems. We have greatly diminished the feelings of guilt and shame attached to adult sexuality. But we have gone to the extreme of removing all limits on sexual expression and exposing children, as well as adults, to sexuality in its most intimate and perverse aspects. Our children are sexually overexposed and overstimulated. They are seduced into adult personality, both in the house and outside, before they are mature enough to handle those feelings. And they are forced to cut off their sexual feelings so as not to be overwhelmed by the stimulation. They grow up without a conscious sense of guilt about sexuality, but with great fear of any overwhelming sexual passion.

Victorian people were restricted in sexual expression, though they had strong feelings. We suffer from a lack of feeling, though sexual expression is open. To put it simply, we have become a people without passion and, therefore, without real pleasure in life. Instead we are power oriented, like the machines that create our culture. Power, productivity and publicity are the dominant forces in our culture—all measured by the dollar sign.

Those of us, like myself, who are clinically involved in the problems of human beings recognize that there has been a deterioration in the personality of people who come for therapy. The kind of neurotic personalities that Freud described, and which I saw in my early years as a therapist, are not so evident today. We see more people who suffer from a schizoid condition of loss of identity, alienation, lack of feelings and depersonalization. And the bodies of people who come to my office, or of those I see in the workshops I do around the world, show a similar disintegration. They are less integrated, show more distortions, and are less energetically charged. In my opinion the main reason for the surge of interest in the body in the last decade is people's awareness that they have lost their bodies, which they are now trying to find.

If we wish to reverse the process, we have to understand the forces in human nature that made such a situation possible. Since civilization began, man has struggled to understand his own nature. Prior to civilization there was no such need. Man lived in harmony with nature—the nature within and without him—like all the other animals. There was no struggle and no torment. Man lived in the Garden of Eden, the earthly paradise. He lived in the bliss of ignorance. This state ended when he was tempted and ate the fruit of the tree of knowledge. Then he became like God, knowing good from evil. His state of bliss ended. He was expelled from the Garden of Eden.

I could elaborate on this theme. When man ate the forbidden fruit, he fell from grace. The Bible says God was angry. Man fell from God's grace. But the word "grace" should be taken literally. Man lost the gracefulness that characterized him in the stage of ignorance, that is, when he was still like the other animals. All wild animals are naturally graceful. Those of us who work with the bodies of people realize how ungraceful most people are. Their movements are uncoordinated. They don't flow. Watch a squirrel racing along the tree tops and you can gain some idea of what natural grace is. Watch the birds fly, the fish swim or the deer run. Only man among God's creatures is ungraceful. He has lost his harmony with his inner being and with nature.

Erich Fromm says it this way: "In the animal there is an uninterrupted chain of reactions starting with a stimulus, like anger, and ending with a more or less strictly determined course of action, which does away with the tension created by the stimulus. In man that chain is interrupted—Instead of a predetermined intuitive action, man has to weigh possible courses of action in his mind; he starts to think. He changes his role toward nature from that of a purely passive adaptation to an active one; he produces. He invents tools and, while thus mastering nature, he separates himself from it more and more."*

The early Greeks had a good understanding of the contradictions in human nature. They knew that the human being was a strange creature. They expressed the puzzle of his nature in

* Erich Fromm, *Escape from Freedom.*

the famous riddle of the Sphinx. The Sphinx was a creature with the head of a woman and the body of a lion. According to Greek mythology, she roamed the outskirts of the city of Thebes. If she caught a traveler to the city, she asked him this conundrum: What creature walks on four legs in the morning, two legs at midday and three legs in the evening? If the traveler failed to answer the question correctly, she devoured him.

We are all familiar with the fact that Oedipus was the famous Greek hero who destroyed the Sphinx by answering the question correctly. His answer was: Man, who in his infancy crawls on all fours, in his maturity walks on two legs, and who in the evening of his life, when he is an old man, has three legs because he walks with a cane. When the Sphinx heard this answer, she threw herself into the sea and was drowned. Oedipus returned to Thebes a hero. He became king of Thebes and married the widowed queen, which was his reward for freeing the city from the monster. It turned out that the queen was his own mother and that, without knowing it, he had killed his own father. Oedipus learned this after he had been married to his mother for twenty years and had four grown children with her. Jocasta, the queen, was so distraught that she killed herself. Oedipus was so shocked by his blindness that he put out his own eyes and became a wanderer on the earth.

In what way was Oedipus blind? He could not have known that the man he killed in a fight on the highway was his own father or that the woman he married was his own mother, since he had been staked out to die when he was born. His blindness was related to his arrogance. He was the smart one who had overcome the Sphinx, but he failed to see that everyman marries his mother. The phallic gods are both the sons and husbands of the great goddess, Mother Earth. The answer that

Oedipus gave to the Sphinx while correct was nevertheless incomplete. Who or what is this strange creature we call man who walks on two legs, three legs and four legs?

As a baby crawling on all fours, the human child is like all other land mammals who go about on four legs. He is born and nourished as they are. At this stage he is simply an animal no different from the other mammals. However, he does not remain in this stage very long. Between his first and and second year he learns to stand and walk on two legs and also to speak. These abilities distinguish man from all other animals. This transformation is not fully completed until the sixth year, when a child loses all his baby teeth. In most cultures it is the age when the indoctrination to adulthood begins. In our culture it is the time when a child starts his formal education. I believe that a child remains closely tied to his animal nature until about six years of age.

What does it mean to be like an animal? First, it means to be fully identified with the body and committed to the immediate satisfaction of bodily needs and desires. Second, it means to live fully in the present. And third, it means to respond freely and spontaneously to all situations without the intervention of rational thought as Fromm described it. Of course this transformation of a child does not take place over night. The child forsakes his animal nature only slowly and gradually, in response to his inner development and under pressure from his parents.

In his upright posture, which frees his hands to manipulate the environment, and in his use of language man is unlike all other animals. Whereas they are part of nature and fully subject to her laws, man can use his knowledge of those laws to act upon and control nature for his benefit. *Homo sapiens* is not only a creature, he is also a creator. On four legs one is oriented downward toward the earth. In the erect posture one's gaze is directed forward to the horizon and upward to the sky. The beginning of civilization and culture is marked everywhere by the study of the heavens. Astronomy was and is man's primary interest. He has always looked upward to the source of his life, the energy of the sun. He conceives of God, which quite early he identified with the sun, as in ancient Egypt. In the next step man begins to identify himself with God. At first this identification is limited to the Pharaoh or ruler with absolute power, but it slowly spreads to others as man gains increasing power over nature through the use of machines. He believes that he is created in the image of God and, therefore, godlike. Over the millennia he has attempted to reach that potential. Jacob Bronowski, in his book *The Ascent of Man*, describes the human being as "lower than the angels." The implication is that with continued effort he may reach godhood.

Consider the attributes we assign to God: omniscience and omnipotence. Man wants to be omniscient and omnipotent. His curious and restless mind is seeking constantly to uncover all nature's secrets. We must recognize that this is the nature of the human mind. It is also in the nature of the human mind to want to be able to do everything it can conceive of. In his mind man would like to overcome the limitations of his finite being, namely, death, illness, gravity. Like Jonathon Livingston Seagull, he wants to transcend his animal nature, to become pure spirit divorced from the flesh.

The practical effect of man's drive to become a god is shown in the work he has done to recreate the world in his own image. The world as God created it is the natural world, a world of blue sky and green earth, a world of clean air and clear water, a world of animals, not machines. Man's world, as we see it about us, is made of gray concrete and yellow smog, of metal and paper, of noise and dirt. Of course not all of man's creations are life destructive. Much that he has created has enriched life. However, he is not a god. His knowledge is only partial compared with the infinity of the universe. And there is nothing more dangerous than a little knowledge. When man plays at being God, he becomes either a lunatic or a monster like the Roman emperor Caligula.

The human dilemma is that man is a creature with a dual aspect, an animal body and a godlike mind. This dilemma cannot be resolved by an either-or position—body or mind, animal or god. There is, however, a third term in the problem. In the evening of his life man is a creature who walks on three legs. He is no longer secure on two legs, he needs the help of a cane. His mortality stares him in the face. He can't continue to reside on Olympian heights. Age has brought him closer to the earth. Then, when his days are over, he will return to the earth like the other animals. One knows in old age that the aspiration to be a god can never be realized, that it is one's fate to be born an animal and to die like one.

The human child, as an animal, lives fully in the present. As an adult, standing on two legs, man looks into the future. To be creative one must plan with an eye to the future and one must sacrifice immediate pleasure for the greater satisfaction that fulfillment of the dream could offer. At the same time one must live in the present, too, or there would be no future. The future exists only in fantasy or dream. But as one becomes old, the future becomes dim. In recompense, the past becomes more vivid, and old people tend to live in the past, without, however, losing consciousness of the present or the future. If that consciousness is lost, one becomes senile.

Just as each of the three stages of man's life has a different relationship to time, so they have a different relationship to mental functioning. The mind of an infant functions largely on the unconscious level; that is to say, an infant is unaware of thought processes. The mind of an animal functions in the same way. Yet this kind of functioning is quite adequate for the needs of an infant or an animal. An infant or animal has an *understanding* of life and life processes which it has gained in the course of a long evolutionary history. This understanding is in the body, which includes the brain. For example, an animal or child doesn't have to study biochemistry to understand how to regulate the acid-base balance of its blood. Its metabolism functions beautifully without any knowledge of the Krebs cycle, amino acids or urea production. An animal never need take a course in sex education to understand how to copulate and reproduce. It has *understanding,* which means that it is guided from below (under). What stands under an animal's behavior is the experience of the past. But it has no knowledge of this past experience.

Knowledge is a function of consciousness, or more accurately, of self-consciousness. It represents the ability to abstract experience into language or other symbols. It has to be acquired anew by each generation, even though we can accumulate it in books or other records; it is a function of the head, that is, of the observing and thinking ego. The striving for knowledge and power characterizes the two-legged stage of man's life, when he aspires to be a god. Knowledge, of course, is power. To an animal or small child both knowledge and power are meaningless. Through knowledge and power man transforms the world.

It would be very nice if our knowledge and our understanding dovetailed, if our knowledge were based upon and grew out of our understanding. Too often, however, the two conflict. We are taught to rely upon knowledge and not upon understanding, because the latter is not objective. For example, every mother intuitively and instinctly understands how to raise a child. Mothers have been doing it from time immemorial and have not needed books on child psychology. But if she reads books or listens to pediatricians, both of whom profess to have knowledge, she no longer trusts her own sensing or sensibility. The result is that she falls from grace, and so does her child. She is bound to mess it up.

What is the nature of mental functioning in an older person? Such a person has gone through the process of giving up understanding to acquire knowledge. Hopefully, he or she has come to the realization that knowledge has no answers. The more we know, the more there is to know. Hopefully, he or she realizes that we never become gods, that while the aspiration to be godlike is noble, the idea that one can be a god is an illusion. Hopefully, he or she has gained *wisdom,* which is the recognition that knowledge without understanding is fool's gold, that power without pleasure is a fool's paradise. *Wisdom* is the ability to look backward, as well as forward, and to see that we all return to the same place in the end. *Wisdom* is to know that life is a journey to be experienced, not a destination to be reached.

One of my associates told me the following story. A young man who had inherited a lot of money set out to discover the meaning of life. He traveled around the world asking all the

philosophers for an explanation of life. No one could give him
an answer that was definitive. After many years of futile search-
ing he learned of a wise old man who lived in the Andes
mountains. I suppose a wise old man lives in the mountains so
he can be free from the busy-ness (business) of life. The young
man made the voyage and finally reached the abode of the old
man. When he was admitted, he said, "Father, I have traveled
far and wide to find what life is about, but no one has been able
to give me an answer. You are my last hope."

The old man replied, "Life is a fountain. It goes up and it
comes down."

The young man was angry and said, "Is that all you can tell
me, after all the trouble I have gone to?"

"Well," answered the old man, "doesn't it?"

It does. Life is a going up and a coming down. It is like a
seesaw or a swing. The excitement is in the going up, but the
pleasure or fulfillment is in the coming down. Down is the
flood of feeling in the belly when the swing drops or the roller
coaster descends. Down is the discharge of sexual excitement
in the orgasm, it is the return home of the hunter or warrior.
Imagine the anxiety if there were no coming down: if the swing
stayed perched in the air, if the roller coaster rested on the
summit, if the sexual release did not occur, if the laborer never
ceased his work nor the warrior his fighting. Even God rested
on the seventh day. But in Los Angeles the beat goes on
twenty-four hours a day, seven days a week. The traffic never
stops, the lights never go out, the city never sleeps. It is enough
to drive one crazy, and that is, in my opinion, what is happening to us.

Down is toward the earth, nature and the body. Up is toward
power, productivity and the psyche. Don't get hung up on the

latter. They add excitement to life if one can come down to BEING in the BODY—and that means accepting one's identity as a HUMAN BEING, and not as a GOD DOING. However, I very much suspect that we will talk about body, feeling and sex as something to DO, rather than as a way of BEING. And I am very much afraid that our culture has pushed us so high up that we cannot come down without a crash.

IDA ROLF

Although she has named it Structural Integration, Ida Rolf's technique for changing the structure of the human body is universally referred to as "Rolfing." Worldwide, there are now over 160 Rolfers, namely, those certified to do Structural Integration, a process of deep muscular massage which, over the course of ten hourly sessions, is designed to render the human body in greater balance within itself and with the field of gravity.

But although Rolfing was specifically conceived of as a way of changing physical structure, Dr. Rolf came to see that these structural changes seemed always to make changes in the way the human functioned. Specifically, Rolfing provoked behavioral changes. Thus, Structural Integration has been, for many persons, an experience of profound psychological change.

Ida Rolf is a New Yorker—born, raised and educated in New York City. She graduated from Barnard College in 1916, a student of chemistry. The First World War had drained off the supply of available male chemists, opening up the unusual possiblity for women chemists to find interesting work. This was the case with Rolf, who was hired by the Rockefeller Institute, where she first did research on antisyphilitics, then later worked with intermediate drugs that were tested for their effectiveness in combating African sleeping sickness.

The Rockefeller Institute provided the research facilities for Rolf to complete her Ph.D. in organic chemistry at Columbia University, after which she was named to the regular staff of the institute, where under Dr. P.A. Levine, she investigated the various constituents of body tissue. Specifically, Dr. Rolf was interested in the chemical structure of lipids, substances comprising the structural bulk of the nervous system.

During the late twenties the Rockefeller Institute sent Rolf to Europe to investigate certain research programs in fermentation. It was during this time that she heard lectures in Zurich by Erwin Schrodinger and Peter Joseph Wilhelm Debys, who fueled her suspicion that human behavior had a dependence on both the body's chemistry and the physics of the body. This led her to more extensive studies in chemistry and physics.

Returning from Europe, she remained with the Rockfeller Institute until 1928, married and had her first son born in 1932. During these family years at Stoney Brook, and later Manhasset, she began applying her knowledge about the changing of bodily structure. One of the first persons she worked on was a piano teacher whose arms had been damaged in an accident.

A strong influence at this time was Ida Rolf's regular attendance at the famous Saturday night meetings of Dr. Pierre Bernard, in Nyack, New York. Bernard's ideas represented a radical departure from the tradition of modern medicine. These controversial ideas expressed the tantric theme of viewing the human being as a whole: body, mind and spirit. It was Bernard's proposal that medicine should seek to integrate these three elements, thus restoring the human to wholeness.

The techniques and theory of Structural Integration developed gradually during this period, and Rolf found a practice developing as well: Friends she had worked with told others, who told still others, and soon the profession of Rolfing was born.

It was not, however, until Richard Price and Michael Murphy heard of her work that Rolfing began to take on the renown which it has today. Price and Murphy invited Rolf to live at the Esalen Institute at Big Sur, where she demonstrated her work, lectured and began to teach others to do it. The irrepressible Fritz Perls was also reigning at Esalen during this same period, and he became a supporter of Rolf's work.

Eventually, The Rolf Institute was formed, with its headquarters in Boulder, Colorado. It is there, and in other centers around the United States, that Dr. Rolf directs the training of new Rolfers.

The ten sessions of Structural Integration are a carefully devised program whereby specific fasciae and muscles of the body are stretched out from their cramped and distorted positions. Each session focuses on different muscles of the body until, by the tenth session, the entire structure of the body has been brought into a state of structural balance and integration.

Although seemingly distant from her original work as an organic chemist, Ida Rolf sees Structural Integration as a clear extension of her original research. In particular, she sees Rolfing as a way in which the overall entropy of the human body is reduced. From this point of view, Rolfing is an antidote to the otherwise irreversible entropic forces described in the Second Law of Thermodynamics.

BIBLIOGRAPHY:

Johnson, Don. *The Protean Body: A Rolfer's View of Human Flexibility.* 1977.
Rolf, Ida. *Rolfing—The Integration of Human Structures.* 1977.

Structure: A New Factor in Understanding the Human Condition

IDA ROLF

WE who nurture human bodies are aware that at present we seem to be operating in a dichotomy, an "old medicine" and a "new medicine." The "newer medicine" has gained its leadership by virtue of the additional factors which it takes into account, one of these being the ever-present environment, a second the consideration of basic physical structure. Both of these factors have been relatively ignored until recently. The "older medicine" seemed to have a certain relation to "magic." It depended on the properties of various "healing" substances introduced into the body and seemingly "magically" efficacious. Some few of these substances were inorganic; many were organic, from mineral, vegetable and animal sources. Introduced into the human body, these produced specific results; sometimes in their apparent irrelevance it looked like magic. The "good" doctor was the man who intuitively knew how to get the greatest relief of symptoms. This was his "magic." At this earlier stage much verbal attention was directed, sometimes very loudly, toward "causes." But in actuality the attention was focused on antecedent conditions. That which had happened just before the symptom appeared was all too often called its cause. In this period, the greater reliance was on the introduction into the living system of something from the outside to effect a curative change.

Humans have been changing this assumption and now tend to believe that the responsibility for healing and curing lies within the individual himself. This may almost be regarded as the hallmark of the "new medicine." We now say it has been the individual's error which introduced the problem; it must be his responsibility to recognize the error, correct it and thus remedy the condition. In short, modern thinking places the responsibility for his well-being squarely within the suffering individual, and very often within his mental approach to life. It categorically denies the efficacy of the "Little Green Devils" feared by our ancestors.

With the entry of the therapies of Still (of osteopathy) and Palmer (of chiropractic), therapists began to look for something they felt was more truly a cause. It was from the searchings of these men and, later, their followers that the idea was introduced that physical structure, its order or disorder, might have a great basic significance as cause. In response to this search for causes, and with the identification of structure as a possible contributing factor, the "newer medicine" used manipulation as the logical means to modify structure. This type of intervention has been tremendously successful in many places, but it was still recognized, especially by its practitioners, that something more was needed.

Let us look at this added premise, the idea of structure. There are many ideas about structure. Used in a material connotation the word implies the presence of space: the three dimensions of ordinary space, or sometimes the four dimensions of space/time. Therefore, it is apparent that structure always implies relationship. The dictionary definition of structure is "the interrelation of parts or the principle of organization in a complex entity" (American Heritage Dictionary). Thus the concept is never absolute, it is necessarily relative. Sometimes the relationship implied is between material particles, sometimes between the changes undergone by material particles in time.

The word structure is not limited to matter; it can also apply to ideas. But the kind of structure which we are considering here has to do with the sort of energy aggregates which constitute the matter of our material world. Meditation on "structure" gives rise to some very strange insights. We see that even in the densest material an energy system is basic, and therefore, the system has attributes which can be called behavior. In all living systems, structure manifests itself in behavior. We might say, in a sense, structure actually is behavior. This is true at any level of matter, be it organic, inorganic or vital.

What does all this philosophy have to do with life in Los Angeles, New York, San Francisco or Chicago? Actually a very great deal. What we have implied up to now is that badly misplaced or malformed structure might be expected to result in unfortunate behavior. Here we must remember that we are using the word behavior not merely in the ordinary sense of human conduct, but to designate the full range of what any material system expresses or is able to demonstrate. Thus, the "behavior" of salt includes the elevation of the boiling point of water when it is dissolved in water. When we see a man unfortunately deformed in either gross structure or mien, we may well consider that here is evidence of a situation which may well result in possible poor behavior. By the term poor or bad behavior we ordinarily mean that he uses violent or otherwise inappropriate conduct to obtain his ends. But in accordance with this newer viewpoint, it is more appropriate to say that part or parts of his body are not functioning properly, and the outward manifestation of this is, as we call it, poor behavior. So as we go around the streets of our cities, our towns, our homes, we may look around us with newly seeing eyes and more understanding hearts at the visible evidences of poor structure manifesting as behavior, sometimes physical, sometimes mental, sometimes emotional.

All of this offers interesting material for observation, but what does it mean to us as therapists? To us who call ourselves Structural Integrationists and who by our friends are sometimes called Rolfers, it means something very dear to our hearts; it means hope. For we know that we Rolfers are able to change body structure. We can change body structure in a way and to a degree which up to the relatively present time has not been thought possible. We know that we can direct and change the body toward a balanced vertical. As we look at what has been added when such a change has been made we are suddenly and startlingly aware that we, in practicing the Rolf process, have been dealing, even though unconsciously, with the great energy field of the earth, which we call gravity, in addition to the more obvious smaller field of the individual, which people have always expected to be able to influence to a degree. As we change the physical body, the energy field, of the man, the larger field of the earth is able to act differently on the smaller energy field of the individual.

In considering this we find certain assumptions helpful for our understanding of what we see. One such assumption tells us we are taking into account a more comprehensive view of man than was included in the purely Aristotelian definition of *Homo sapiens*. Here we must see man as an energy field, rather than as a mass of matter—a field which lives within a greater energy field, the field of the earth. These two fields, like any two energy fields, necessarily interact. In any competition the greater field of the earth will necessarily win. There is an old "Peanuts" cartoon which I love. Linus is meditating having just seen Lucy fall down and come up crying. He reflects: "For hundreds of years there have been sidewalks, for hundreds of years there have been little girls. The little girls are always falling on the sidewalks. The sidewalks always win."

This last sentence sums up everything I have said up to now: The gravity field always wins. But this purely intellectual discussion fails to take note that—realistically—in winning, the larger field, the environment, steadily undermines the integrity of the smaller field. If there is no appropriate intervention, this undermining will continue to a point of eventual breakdown in the smaller field. But fortunately there is a hopeful aspect in this rather grim situation. There is the happy possibility that we can restore the undermined structure, because incredibly, the human body is so outstandingly a plastic medium. As Rolfers, we use this fact to great and unexpected advantage.

The definition of plastic is a substance which under stress of pressure can be deformed and on release of the stress can be restored to its original state. This is the message proclaimed by Structural Integration, one important system of which is called Rolfing. Any real integration (including Rolfing) must concern itself not merely with the structure of the body as such, but also with the structure of the body and, simultaneously, with the effect and influence of its energy environment, the gravitational field, on that structure. In school you were probably taught that all the chronic ills of a human came from his attempt to stand on two legs instead of on the four for which they told you he was originally designed. But man is a species that is emerging, not static. He is emerging inexorably toward verticality, and when he reaches verticality the energy of the earth's field automatically supports him, adding to his personal energy, and he reports this in all his "behavior": how he feels, how he stands, how he walks, how he acts, how he digests, how he thinks, how he relates to the world and to his fears and his feelings.

As Rolfers we know that through a combination of manipulation and, particularly, of education in understanding the use of his body and its movements, we can bring any human to a more nearly vertical stance. The structural support of a man is in his collagen, his myofascial system—fasciae, tendons, ligaments, bones. It is because of the unique chemical and physical properties of collagen that we are able to bring man toward the vertical. At this position of verticality gravitational forces reinforce him, because at the surface of the earth, gravity acts as a set of vertical lines. Gravity no longer tears him down or pulls him apart. Then he says, "I feel good. I feel wonderful. What have you done to me?" But it is not we who have created this well-being, it is gravity.

Gravity, man's name for the energy of the earth, is the never-sleeping therapist and teacher. All that we men and women as Rolfers can do is to prepare the body of the individual to receive and respond positively to the effects of the gravitational field. This is our sole contribution. And therein is the message of structure.

CHARLOTTE SELVER & CHARLES BROOKS

When Alan Watts first described the work of Charlotte Selver, he said, "Charlotte, what you are doing is *living Zen!*" As much as anything, this characterizes the high spirituality, as well as high presence of mind, taught by Charlotte Selver.

What she teaches is called Sensory Awareness, and she teaches it with her colleague and husband, Charles Brooks. Not accidentally, they live next to the Zen Buddhist Farm that is located just north of San Francisco. Richard Baker Roshi, who is Director of the Zen Center, has this to say about them:

"The work which Charlotte Selver and Charles V. W. Brooks do cannot be described in words—it is the language of our spirit and being. They are among the greatest guides I know to the new or forgotten world in which mind and body are one."

This "new or forgotten world" is the somatic world—a realm in which self-awareness is the same as a body-being-aware-of-it-self. Most especially, it is a realm in which self-awareness can grow, and this growth in the range of self-awareness is, automatically, a simultaneous growth in the integrity and balance of our physiological system. The *gnosis* of our sensory brain tracts is inescapably linked with the *praxis* of our motor neural system: somatically, "to know is to do." In sum, growth in self-knowledge is equivalent with growth in self-control, thus being a way for the human being to better integrate (i.e., have a more efficient central neural command of) the millions of internal movements which go on in his or her body every second.

That self-awareness leads to self-control is nowhere better illustrated than in the life of Elsa Gindler, the celebrated Berlin physical educator who was Charlotte's teacher. As a young woman, Gindler was stricken with tuberculosis in one of her lungs. Unable to afford the medical treatment of collapsing and resting the lung at a Swiss sanatorium, Gindler decided to do an unheard-of thing: She would cease breathing in the affected lung, directing all of her breathing through the good lung. She managed to do this so successfully that the lung recovered and healed.

The implications of this—self-awareness creates self-control— were explored throughout her life by Gindler and her many pupils. In ever varying ways, she invited her pupils to become aware of themselves in, for example, walking: How are your feet hitting the ground? What are your shoulders doing? What is the rhythm of your breathing while walking? Feel the air move across your skin as you walk.

Because it dealt with the characteristically human ability to switch points of view and to differentiate awareness, Gindler called her work *Arbeit am Menschen* (work on people). Selver studied a number of years with Gindler, as she also did with the Swiss experimental educator Heinrich Jacoby. For both of these teachers, says Selver, "the main thing . . . was to become genuine again, to come to one's original capacities and cultivate *them* rather than being taught to do things in a particular way." This is the somatic view: that human life being a process, the first concern is to improve the process itself.

It was in 1938 that Charlotte Selver came to the United States, where she spent a number of years in New York, developing her own manner of teaching movement sensitivity. She called it Sensory

Awareness, and its strong influence on other figures of the time is rooted in the fact that it introduces learners to the world of their immediate experience, a realm stripped of its verbal wrappings. In a certain manner, Sensory Awareness induces awareness of the preverbal world of infanthood, a time when the total content of consciousness is of sensing and moving.

It was this world into which she introduced Erich Fromm, expanding his appreciation of the nonverbal, unconscious aspects of human experience. Through her work with the wife of Wilhelm Reich, the latter came to adopt breathing exercises into his therapeutic techniques. She taught Sensory Awareness to Fritz Perls, who subsequently included it in the variety of procedures he later called Gestalt psychology. And as mentioned, her work had a special significance to Alan Watts, who taught Selver that the presumably European tradition of Sensory Awareness was indistinguishable from much of the Asian tradition of Zen Buddhism.

Charles Brooks has, for many years, been not only co-partner in teaching Sensory Awareness but also the spokesman for this subtle teaching. With talents not unexpected from one who is the son of Van Wyck Brooks, Charles Brooks has rendered the insights of Gindler-Selver into prose that is as lucid as it is sun filled. Together, Selver and Brooks are luminous guides to a realm where body and mind coalesce into a self-awareness that is, at once, sensual and spiritual.

BIBLIOGRAPHY

Brooks, Charles V. W. *Sensory Awareness: The Rediscovery of Experiencing,* 1974.

Notes About the Human Potential

CHARLOTTE SELVER
AND CHARLES BROOKS

WHEN I am asked to say what I believe to be the nature of the human being I answer that the full range of our potentials has never been consciously discovered by us and lies as yet unused, but can be brought to life and gradually unfolded; that what we *do* use we often use to disadvantage with regard to our energy expenditure (and subsequently to our functioning), as well as with regard to the quality of our actions; and finally, that there are *no ungifted people!* If we believe we are ungifted, we will find on closer examination that we are only *hindered,* and hindrances can gradually be shed when we get insight into what has held us back, and we can give ourselves new chances—what I might call a fresh learning.

This capacity for learning, which extends so much farther in us than in other creatures, is—it seems to me—the noblest gift man has at his disposal; but while his greatest asset, it is also his greatest danger. The marvelous process by which we come to stand and to speak, to form shapes and rhythms, to analyze, calculate and organize is in its very flexibility and versatility peculiarly liable to deformation. This is why education has such importance for everyone.

Zen Buddhism and Taoism teach that if we would allow the giving up of the effects of previous conditioning and become again able to experience and unfold our untapped potentials, only then would we live *normally*—that is, according to our actual human design. What we usually call "normal" is far from our rich human possibilities.

What is this thing, which some people seem to have and to which we always feel strangely attracted? Such people seem to live lives of great inner richness. I saw this quality at work when I watched a friend—a delicate, fragile woman of more than eighty years of age—giving a treatment to a patient for well over one and a half hours. After she was done, the patient, wonderfully relieved, exclaimed, "From where do you have this strength and this marvelous sensitivity?"

My friend smiled at her and answered, "Everybody has it, only we don't know about it!"

If we all have it, and yet don't seem to have it, what has happened? Where is it hidden? It must be locked up. What has created this locking up?

The two chief enemies of fuller functioning are *fear* and *conditioning*. The effects of fear and conditioning begin the first moment we arrive in this world, if not already before. Feldenkrais says:

> A newborn infant is practically insensitive to external stimuli. At birth he hardly reacts to light effects, to noise, smell and even moderate pinching. He reacts violently to immersion in very cold or hot water. Also if suddenly lowered, or if support is sharply

withdrawn, a violent contraction of all flexors with halt of breath is observed, followed by crying, accelerated pulse and general vasomotor disturbance. *The similarity of reaction of a newborn infant to withdrawal of support, and that of fright or fear in the adult, is remarkable. . . .*

Anxiety in whatever form must be related to the inborn response to falling. Every shock or emotional disturbance, for whatever reason it may happen, is—symbolically speaking—created through a withdrawal of support: the floor, so to speak, is being pulled out from under our feet. Hence the similarity of protective reaction: FEAR, contraction; DEFENSE, contraction; RESISTANCE, contraction; and so on. So we see that fear in all cases leads to contraction and withdrawal of the organism. And if this fear becomes habitual, we have conditioning, for conditioning—as I use the term—is the antithesis of free, full functioning in the human being.

The newborn infant has more than just an inborn reaction of fear to loss of support: When he feels safe and supported he naturally responds with interest and curiosity to the world around him. I could not say it better than Ernst Schachtel. Some years ago he wrote about this:

It is safe to assume that early childhood is the period of human life which is richer in experience. Everything is new to the newborn child. . . . No Columbus, no Marco Polo has ever seen stranger and more fascinating and thoroughly absorbing sights than the child that learns to perceive, to taste, to smell, to touch, to hear and to see, and to use his body, his senses, and his mind. No wonder that the child shows an insatiable curiosity. He has the whole world to discover. Education and learning, while on the one hand furthering this process of discovery, on the other hand gradually brake and finally stop it completely. There are relatively few adults who are fortunate enough to have retained something of the child's curiosity, his capacity for questioning and for wondering. The average adult . . . has ceased to wonder, to discover. . . . It is this adult who answers the child's questions and, in answering, fails to answer them, but instead acquaints the child with the conventional patterns of his civilization, which effectively close up the asking mouth and shut the wondering eye. . . .

But he continues:

Even if, in modern western civilization, the capacity for such fresh experience has largely been deadened, most people, unless they have become complete automatons, have had glimpses of the exhilarating quality that makes fresh experience, unlabeled, so unique, concrete and filled with life.*

For it is true that *interest fires the tissues.* Vitality, nerve activity, organic functioning, reactivity, are at their best when we are really interested and in contact with what we are doing. Senses are open for reception, muscles for necessary changes, energy supply is at hand just as we need it; we are ready for action just as for rest—whatever is warranted. Our whole self functions in what we do.

But when our thirst for genuine experience is more and more discouraged, vitality tends to ebb away or is wasted by continued repression. Every function becomes lowered in its power. Increasingly the stimulation, which objects of interest could create, diminishes. We become more and more *constricted,* or—on account of the unsatisfied hunger for the needed stimulus—we become restless.

---

* Ernst Schachtel, the great expert in the Rorschach test, was one of my students. One day when we worked on sensing, he suddenly exclaimed, "I have written about this—I never experienced it!" (I was amazed at his honesty.)

Genuine, natural experience arises basically from and through our sensory equipment, and it is the loss of connection with our simple, subtle senses which diminishes all subsequent functioning of the organism. Schachtel says:

> The infant, long before he knows and remembers how his mother looks, knows how she smells and tastes. Very likely, angry or frightened mother tastes and smells rather different from good or comfortable mother to the infant, just as she will look very different to him as he grows older. In his growing experience of the world around him, the proximity senses (touch, taste, smell) at first have primacy over the distance senses (seeing, hearing). In order to get really acquainted with something or somebody, he has to touch it and put it in his mouth as he first did with his mother's nipple. Only very gradually and slowly does the emphasis shift from the proximity to the distance senses. This . . . shift is helped along powerfully and the development of taste and smell discouraged by the stringent taboos of the significant adults. . . .

As the child grows, more and more taboos await him or her. Let me give you a small example. I was visiting friends in their home one day. Among the guests there was a couple with their daughter, a little girl of eight—a thoughtful and very graceful child. While we were talking, the little girl played in the garden. I had the pleasure of watching her through the window. Then she came upstairs and sat down, one leg hanging down, the other one on the couch. The mother said, "But Helen! How do you sit? Take your leg off the couch. A girl never should sit like that!" The little girl took her leg down, at which her skirt flew high above her knees. The mother said, "Helen! Pull your skirt down. One can see everything!" The child blushed, looked down at herself and pulled her skirt down, but asked, "Why? What is wrong?" The mother looked at her quite shocked and said, "One does not do that!" By this time the atmosphere in the room was completely uncomfortable. The little girl not only had her legs down but had them pressed against each other. Her shoulders had gone up, and she held her arms tight against her little body. This went on until she could not stand it any longer; suddenly she stretched herself and yawned heartily. Again a storm of indignation from her mother. By now—this all lasted about ten minutes—the child had changed completely. Her gracefulness had turned into awkwardness; all her motions were stilled, her little body was tense; she hardly seemed to be alive any more.

What will happen to this child? She will hold her unhappy pose for a few minutes before she shakes it off. The next time her mother admonishes her, she will hold it for a few minutes longer—and so on. Each time a little longer, until at last she will have repressed her naturalness so deeply that she will have forgotten it. The mother will then have reached her goal: She will have educated her daughter to be socially acceptable. As a human being the child will be greatly inhibited, for as the mother forms her in this direction, she will also form her in a thousand other directions.

The effects of such shame-induced change is always individual, but changes induced by these means—which many adults seem to find necessary—always create an imbalance, an impoverishment for the child which continues into adulthood. *Conflict* is built into such changes, because spontaneous impulses will try again and again to reestablish nature-given reactivity, which then each time has to be suppressed. Finally it may be that the person has built up such resistance within himself, in the form of constriction or dullness, that he does not feel these natural tendencies any more.

One day my teacher, Elsa Gindler, asked one of the students in her class to experiment alone. He was a famous engineer, totally intellectual, his head burning with intensity, the rest of him as though dead, his skin a yellow-gray. When he moved he toppled; no muscles were recognizable in his thin legs.

He stood against a wall. His task was to lift one of his heels slightly and let it come down to the floor again. Ready to work for hours on his engineering problems, he willingly obliged. We all watched. His movements were fast at first, and Elsa Gindler repeatedly suggested that he take more time to sense the way as he was going up with his heel and as he was going down—to give up just being interested in down and up.

After a long time some changes began to be visible. Gradually, movement appeared in the previously wooden, constricted muscles in his leg: The muscles could be seen, they became rounder. They began to slide, one could see extension and contraction. The color of the leg changed from the dead yellowish to a faint rose. I felt tears welling up in me as I witnessed all this happening.

At last Gindler asked him to stop. There he stood, with his two legs as different as night and day, as decay and life.

"What do you feel?" she asked the man. He stood for a while and shook his head. "Do you notice any difference between your two legs?" she asked. He hesitated again; then he said, "No." I could have killed him! Gindler smiled and said, "Not yet, not yet." Wilhelm Reich has spoken eloquently of the "muscle armor" we build against the "danger" of such natural and spontaneous reactions.

The more estranged the educators themselves are from their own bodies, the more they will teach fear- and disgust-inducing taboos; and the greater the fear and disgust so induced, the more will the child become alienated from himself and his environment. His *sense of self* will grow vague and diffuse, opening him continually more to the conditioning of others. This insecurity, so subtly developed ("I don't know; the others know"), follows us through life, weakening our productive abilities more and more. I meet in my classes this dependence, this stern belief in what others advise or teach, no matter how superficial or artificial it might be. It requires a great deal of work to loosen these ties so that we begin to dare again to trust our own sensations and feelings.

Heinrich Jacoby has spelled out what the child learns in an educative process where spontaneity and natural development are ignored:

> First, he no longer trusts his own judgment; he has to be told. Second, the more exactly he repeats, the better. Third, the more he can give the "right" answer, the better a child or student he is. Fourth, the more quickly he thinks and answers, the more intelligent he is judged to be. Fifth, the more effort he makes, the more he will succeed.

Can you feel what all this does to the organism and what attitudes it creates in us? We become directed mainly towards DOING and GETTING and GAINING APPROVAL and MAKING AN EFFORT and FOLLOWING SUPERIM-POSED ADVICE. And where is there room left for INDE-PENDENT DISCOVERING, for the blessing of just BEING, EXISTING, RESPONDING IN A GENUINE WAY, for SENSITIVE AWARENESS?

Helen Keller, blind, deaf and inarticulate from an early age, said this about sensory education:

In order to attain his highest education [the child] must be persistently encouraged to extract joy and constructive interest from sight, hearing, touch, smell and taste. . . . If a mother puts as much gentle art into this delicate fostering of all his physical powers as she does into the task of preserving his health . . . not only will he reach a well-ordered stewardship of his senses, he will also have the best chance of spiritual maturity. . . . Every person, every group thus excellently equipped for living, is the greatest possible contribution to humanity.

So it seems that the only real significance in using our faculties lies in the *quality with which we use them.* This means that superimposed education will have to be laid aside if we are to return to those abilities which nature has given us. We have to rediscover them. We have to learn anew—like children— to use our biological potentials. In this process the wisdom inherent in our own bodies can guide us.

We have to take time to explore what it means to be quiet and to rest. We have to rediscover the supporting power of the earth and find that by entrusting ourselves to it we become free for action. As in childhood, obstacles will attract us again; in meeting them we will strengthen. We will begin not to be discouraged when we meet hardship; such occasions may become very productive instead. We will realize that we can learn from even the smallest experience. The organism, whose resources we had not known, who often was a stranger to us, gradually becomes our friend. We actually discover that the organism is WE—our own living self. We are led back to spontaneity, to fresh, undivided experience, and come close to the concentration clearly expressed by a Zen master:

"What is the Tao [the way, the truth]?" asks the disciple.

"Your every-day mind," replies the Master, and he goes on to amplify: "When I am hungry, I eat; when tired, I sleep."

The disciple is puzzled, and asks whether this is not what everybody else does too.

"No," the Master replies, "most people are never wholly in what they are doing; when eating, they may be absent-mindedly preoccupied with a thousand different thoughts and fantasies; when sleeping, they are not sleeping. The supreme mark of the thoroughly integrated man is to be without a divided mind."

BARBARA BROWN

The discoveries of Dr. Barbara Brown are the landmarks of a career that has moved from research pharmacology to psychopharmacology to neurophysiology and psychophysiology. Here are some of those landmarks:

She has developed five new chemical agents, including Kolantyl for the control of gastric ulcers, Decapryn as an antihistaminic agent, and Frenquel, the first anti-L.S.D. drug.

She was the first to discover the fact that humans move their eyes when trying to remember nonvisual facts.

She was the first to demonstrate that the effects of drugs vary according to personality differences.

She was one of the first scientists to discover that individuals can control their own brain electrical activity.

She was the organizer of the Biofeedback Research Society and was its first president.

She has written two classic works on the expanding field of biofeedback: *New Mind, New Body* and *Stress and the Art of Biofeedback.*

Formerly associated with the UCLA Medical School and the Sepulveda Veterans Hospital, Dr. Brown now resides in Beverly Hills, where she is engaged in purely private research and writing—an independent situation which she fiercely enjoys. She is in no sense a conservative member of the scientific establishment, although she is in every sense highly respected by that establishment for her achievements and her judgment.

A powerful stimulus to Barbara Brown's speculations about the human mind is the extensive exploration she has made of the phenomenon of biofeedback. Biofeedback involves the use of electronic monitors to pick up signals of specific happenings in the body (brain waves, skin temperature, muscular tension, blood pressure, and so on) and to play these signals back (this is the "feedback") to that same person, so that he becomes aware of what his body is doing. For example, persons with chronic hypertension of muscles are, normally, unaware of what their muscles are doing; but by watching feedback from electrodes placed on the forehead—whose frontalis muscle normally contracts when there is tension—the person becomes aware of when the forehead is contracted. Gradually, that person can learn to relax all of his body, using the relaxation of his forehead as a guide.

Both theoretically and practically, the excitement over biofeedback is that it shows that given the correct information about his body, a human is capable of controlling his body. And it is Brown's belief that the human is capable of controlling any aspect of his bodily functions. Charlotte Selver, Charles Brooks and Moshe Feldenkrais all have similar viewpoints.

This is a discovery that has led her into pathways that transcend the normal purview of science, specifically, into the yogic practices of the great Indian swamis and the phenomena of altered states of consciousness. As will become abundantly clear in the following essay, Barbara Brown sees the human mind as a powerful, semi-independent force that can be directed to the transformation of physiological structure.

Biofeedback research suggests that the human mind can be focused upon innumerable bodily functions and that if there is some reliable signal (a flashing light or a buzzer) of a particular bodily function, the mind can obtain greater control of that function. On the surface, this indicates that mind has control over matter—a proposition that is theoretically inadmissible to the canons of science. Yet it is exactly this proposition that seems inescapable to Dr. Brown. In the present essay she propounds a series of what she jocularly calls "Brown's laws," and these are laws that apply to the workings of "Supermind."

Within the past two decades much has been alleged about human potential. The claim has been that, by birthright, every human individual is capable of immensely more than he or others believe. Many of these claims have been confirmed and have been added to our store of knowledge about self-improvement. But all of the confirmed claims are as nothing in comparison with what Barbara Brown suggests in this article. She has brought the tools and thinking of hard science into the arena of human consciousness, and she has made discoveries whose implications are startling: To understand mind at all is to understand that it is supermind.

BIBLIOGRAPHY

1———.and Klug, J. W. *The Alpha Syllabus,* 1974.
2———. *The Biofeedback Syllabus,* 1975.
3———.*New Mind, New Body. Biofeedback: New Directions for the Mind,* 1975.
4———.*Stress and the Art of Biofeedback,* 1977.

On the Nature of
the Human Mind

BARBARA BROWN

I AM going to describe my views on the nature of man by listing the articles for what might be called "A Proclamation for the Emancipation of Mind." I have evolved a series of fundamental principles about the mind of man which, to tickle my ego, I call Brown's Laws, but which perhaps might better be called Laws of Supermind. I don't mean to equate Brown with supermind—but then again, why not? No one else will.

I use the word laws in one of its basic definitions, meaning that laws are statements about natural phenomena which, so far as is known, are invariable.

The laws describe what I have deduced, from considerable scientific evidence, to be some of the fundamental features of the human mind, and from the evidence and laws, I have made two major conclusions: one, that the intellectual apparatus of man is a totally new creation in the evolution of life forms and two, that mind is an energy of brain capable of functioning independently of brain, although born of it and sustained by the physical activity of the brain.

I believe that as modern civilizations evolve, so also simultaneously evolves supermind. Here and there in the recorded history of man we see evidence of these kinds of mind that appear to maximize the mind's abilities for thought, for insights, for intuition, analysis, synthesis and creativity. I believe, moreover, that a similar potential to maximize and expand the functions of mind exists in every human mind as either latent and unrealized or active but frustrated capabilities. Any failure of supermind to emerge as the dominant characteristic of the human species may well be the result of man's own fear that the most potent force of the universe may lie within his own mind. Certainly science has paradoxically renounced the notion of a mind that can function independently of its own physical substrate, and as a consequence, science has failed utterly to investigate the qualities of mind that make the species *Homo sapiens*.

The laws of the human potential I have drawn up describe properties of the human mind that much of the expert knowledge of science has been blind to for much too long. If any scientists disagree with me, they do so *not* on the basis of fact, but from a prejudice that comes from experience limited to too specialized areas of study rather than from comprehensive study of the multiple facets of human life.

Law One: Human beings possess an innate awareness of the state of their biological being, from the total physical body image down to a single cell.

I call this biological awareness and classify it as a specific component of the consciousness spectrum, but a consciousness that is subjectively, privately appreciated only and an awareness that is not ordinarily accessible for objective description.

Nearly every human being has proof of this kind of awareness. Think about your sensations when you try to change the part in your hair. Most people have either a natural part or one they have become used to, and when they try to part the hair in a different place, there is distinct discomfort. It is an awareness that something in the head area doesn't feel quite right, but the exact sensation is almost impossible to describe.

One of the most extraordinary examples of biological awareness was related to me by a friend who is a neurologist and electroencephalographer and who does brain-wave biofeedback. A small, seven-year-old girl, believed to be a mental retardate, was referred to him for diagnosis of her seizures. My friend wired the whole head for recording the EEG, and then, just because his biofeedback equipment was there, the child could watch the complex EEG being written out on a TV monitor in front of her. For the first ten minutes of the recording the brain waves were normal, then, almost buried in the complicated EEG scribbles, there appeared a small abnormal brain wave. The child put her hand to her mouth and whispered, "Oh, excuse me." She had felt her body make a mistake.

This exquisite sensitivity to the hidden functions of one's body is almost too bewildering for us to appreciate fully. Yet other biofeedback studies have repeatedly demonstrated that people can readily become aware of the activity even of single cells once they learn something about how those cells behave.

Law Two: Human beings possess an innate ability to form complex, abstract concepts from primal sensory data.

The story of Helen Keller, the famous blind, deaf mute who attained extraordinary intellectual heights, is the only real example we need to verify this law. When the child Helen Keller was seven, after the turmoil and distress of an intellectually deprived childhood, she was given a tutor. The tutor began by spelling out the letters of words standing for objects she gave the child to feel and touch. In less than two weeks the child had not just learned the word-object associations, but most remarkably, she had also formed several complicated concepts about the structure and organization of language.

Suppose you touch something squishy in the dark. Immediately you call up from memory the information you need to identify the squishy thing, and mainly from touch you form a concept about what the thing most likely is.

A friend of mine had a cousin who, as a child, was judged to be mentally retarded. The parents refused to believe it, and after some effort, they discovered the child could learn quite well through the tactile and kinesthetic senses. The child ultimately became a chemist and won one of the country's most valued prizes for scientific achievement.

Such observations suggest that there is a generally unused mechanism of the intellect capable of forming valid conclusions about the nature of the universe from raw sensory information. This capacity may explain why we begin to understand more about our world when we take the time to contemplate nature itself.

Law Three: Human beings possess an innate ability to exert control over the direction and flow of nerve impulses in any body nerve they choose.

The proof of this law is obvious. Take intentional relaxation and its opposite, purposeful physical activity. In the first case, when you intentionally relax, you voluntarily *decrease* the rate of flow of nerve impulses to the muscles and viscera, while in the second case, physical activity, you intentionally *increase* the rate of flow and specific direction of impulses in the nerves of your choosing.

Scientific proof comes from biofeedback, the process of learning control over body functions. In stress disorders, such as emotional or psychosomatic problems, there is a generalized neural hyperactivity causing the muscles and viscera to be uptight. Using biofeedback learning or any relaxation technique, you learn voluntarily to slow the rate of nerve impulses and direct them toward a specific physiological function. The opposite activity—increasing the rate of flow of nerve impulses —is easily learned, as in rehabilitating muscles paralyzed following a stroke. Here the patient learns how to speed up the flow of nerve impulses to the muscles.

The implications of this law are so great they are almost beyond comprehension. The nervous system, and that includes the brain, implements every action, every function and every thought of human beings. The inborn ability to control all nerve activity means that man has the potential to prevent the malfunction of body activities, the potential to nourish and enhance mental capacities and the potential to correct disordered body functions—in effect, to improve the human condition. This, in fact, is the meaning of Law Four.

Law Four: The human mind has the innate ability to supervene in and direct the physical activities of every physiological function of the body, within the limits of physical nature.

The scientific evidence comes from the success of all the new awareness techniques being used today, all the body awareness techniques, biofeedback and also many psychological procedures, such as imagery. We now know, contrary to previous biomedical beliefs, that human beings can learn, within physical limits, to regulate virtually any body function, from gastric acid secretion to skin electrical activity to the size of blood vessels. And we have finally verified what yogis have known for five thousand years, their ability to control nearly any body function they choose.

The ability of the mind to exert absolute control over body functions can also occur without any conscious awareness. This phenomenon has been demonstrated endlessly under hypnosis. When the hypnotist instructs the subject not to bleed when a needle is thrust into the hand, the subject intentionally but unconsciously prevents bleeding.

Now that we have widespread proof for this law (that mind can control physiological functions), there should be no further excuse for the therapeutic communities not to implement it. Unfortunately we also have politics in science.

Law Five: The mind of human beings can control the physical activities of the brain.

One of the clearest examples of this ability is learning to control brain-wave activity, such as learning to control alpha waves. Alpha activity is a complex activity of the brain neurons, and a physiological activity for which it is completely impossible to have any prior sensory experience whatsoever. You can't see, hear, feel, touch or smell brain waves. Yet people easily learn how to control alpha brain-wave activity by using instruments in which alpha waves are represented by lights or tones. When one uses light or tone signals to learn how to control alpha waves, it is the mind controlling the activity of the brain.

The ultimate control of brain by mind is, of course, thinking. During thinking, the mind must direct a search of memory—both for relevant information and for the appropriate logic to process the information—as well as reject inappropriate, non-relevant information and shunt it away from thought activity. Thinking is voluntary control of the brain.

Law Six: All diseases of society originate in the intellectual processes of man.

Diseases of society are the emotional and physical disorders of man produced by the stress of life. These are the disorders —such as neuroses, hypertension, headaches, ulcers, asthma, insomnia, drug abuse and some fifty other disturbances of functions—that comprise some seventy-five percent of all human illness. Biomedical theory has a weak explanation, believing stress causes arousal of the primitive physical defense mechanisms of man, particularly muscles and viscera. The implication is that human beings react to stress as instinctively as animals to threats to their physical well-being and survival.

I contend that reactions to the stresses of life begin with absolutely normal intellectual activity, that when a person feels stressed, it is because he detects, consciously or unconsciously, a problem somewhere in his social environment. And when one detects a problem in social activities and social relationships, one begins to worry, and with good reason. Worry is a normal problem-solving activity. Emotional problems and physical problems of an emotional origin occur only when the intellectual problem-solving processes are frustrated for any of many reasons. *Not* being able to solve one's social difficulties is a threat to well-being.

We worry when we seem to be unable to resolve problems in social relationships or in our social environments, and when problem solving fails or is frustrated, we can develop any of the well-known behaviors we call emotional: apprehension, anxiety, feelings of inadequacy and of insecurity, uncertainty, frustration, irritation, hostility, loss of self-esteem, and related emotions.

All of these emotions are rooted in an intellectual concern,

concern about social activities, about adequate social perform-
ance, about meeting social criteria and about ensuring one's
social well-being and social survival. The subjective sensations
we call emotions are all expressions of a disturbed intellect, a
disturbance of the intellect about the way social relationships
are perceived and appreciated and interpreted. Stress, in a
word, is manufactured by the intellectual systems of man.
What he needs to relieve the stress is information to solve the
problems.

There is a corollary to this law that stress disorders are a
matter of the intellect. The corollary is that the universal
disease of society is the distress of being sick from any cause
and from what I call "the second illness."

The second illness is the stress of being ill. The stress of
being ill comes from the intellectual appreciation of the loss of
capacity to perform, to participate in life's activities, the loss
of capacity to behave as a normal human being. When we are
sick—emotionally or physically—from any cause, we are socially disadvantaged. Being even the slightest out of the main-
stream of life is stressful.

It is my hope that when we recognize the universal preva-
lence of the second illness, we will begin to treat this as the real
illness it is, and in doing so we can relieve this distress and
speed recovery from the primary illness.

Law Seven: Man has evolved new, sophisticated senses
within the unconscious mind. One of these is the sense of
order.

That is, man possesses a sense that can anticipate (project)
the order of events and sequences of all natural events to move
from chaos and disorder to a naturally ordered, unified result.

A sense of order can be deduced from the evidence that

disorder occurs in the unconscious mind in different states of consciousness, such as the disorder of dream logic, the unconscious conflicts and disorder that are manifest as neuroses, or the disordered perceptions under hallucinogens. If the unconscious mind can become disordered, then it must be capable of maintaining order in its normal functioning.

The most dramatic illustration of the sense of order is when people learn to control single cells in the spinal cord. Called motoneurons, these cells control the activity of small groups of muscle cells, even as few as three. Using an instrument to detect and to display the activity of a single motoneuron, virtually anyone can learn to control the activity of that cell in a few minutes. From watching a light on an instrument to intentionally controlling a single cell is a mind feat of consummate orderliness. Exactly those nerve cells and their connections to accomplish a projected result are selected out of trillions of cell connections and are activated in precise order.

If we accept that human beings do possess such a sense of order, we can better understand how individuals can come to sense and to understand the unifying order of the universe and may become aware of the universal consciousness.

Law Eight: The will of human beings is an independent function of mind, an independently operating energy of mind that decides upon the ordering of biological activity to produce an ordered alteration of the body's functions.

There is no more scientific evidence for the scientific theory that intention, the will, is merely the outcome of mechanical decision-making processes of the brain than there is for concluding that the will is an independently operating function of the mind. The will is the process of mind that makes decisions to act or not to act based on evaluation of the ways to reach the goals and the merits of the goals. Two bits of evidence show the will to be an independent function. One is the fact that the will can be exerted on any body system—muscles, viscera or the central nervous system itself—each of which differs remarkably in chemical and cellular composition, as well as in structure and cell organization. The second bit of evidence is:

Law Nine: In order for the will to act, another independently operating function of mind, a coordinating director or will executor, is required to turn volition into action.

The will executor anticipates the goals and selects the correct channels of neural networks to put into effect the intended action and to produce the change in body activity.

My favorite example of the need of the will for an executor is the time when, in a hurry for a cup of coffee, I found the sugar bowl empty. Grabbing the sack of sugar, I promptly poured it into my coffee. The intention was present, but the executor of the will was out to lunch.

Law Ten: Man has evolved elaborate, as yet unrecognized intellectual mechanisms to ensure his survival in an evolving *nonphysical* environment.

The biomedical, psychological, anthropological and related sciences tend to view man as surviving largely because of various innate, instinctual, inherited physical mechanisms that organisms use to defend against threats to physical well-being. One of the major mechanisms is held by science to be the fight-or-flight response to danger.

I argue that man has his physical environment rather well under control and the need for physical defense mechanisms is rare. What threatens modern man's well-being and survival are primarily the result of the mental activity of other men (here's where I defend male chauvinism; let them take the blame, not women).

It is utterly inappropriate and incongruous for intelligent man to depend upon body mechanisms useful only to defend against threats to physical well-being when it is the malfunctioning of the society of man that threatens man's existence.

The two major sources of danger for modern man are psychological and social. Either ordinary human beings cause psychological problems for other human beings, or dominating hierarchies of human beings in all manner of organized human activities, from the local P.T.A. to the government, cause both psychological and social problems for man.

If we look closely at the direction of many human activities today, we can see the rapidly accelerating evolution of mechanisms of the intellect directed toward ensuring social well-being. One has only to look to the new techniques in psychology and counseling to see that it is the mind that is being evoked as man's primary survival tool. And we in California have Proposition 13 to remind us of ways to deal with social problems we once believed almost beyond our control.

Law Eleven: The highest-order intellectual capacities of man reside in, and may always reside in, what we call the unconscious. That is, unconscious mental processes are elegant, sophisticated and of superior intellect, but they are also unrecognized by society and are untapped human potential.

The most dramatic example of this comes from emotional pathology: hysterical blindness. I personally witnessed such a case in a college friend. The girl was popular on campus, very pretty and quite a good student. One day, about two weeks before finals for the year, she suddenly became blind. In the hospital, the diagnosis finally came down: hysterical blindness.

It doesn't take much more than common sense to reconstruct what must have happened in the mind of this girl, and what similar kinds of mental operations likely happen in all cases of neurosis or psychosomatic illness. Briefly, the girl came to believe that she might not be able to continue her high achievement level in the upcoming final exams, and her solution was to create, quite unconsciously, an apparently foolproof defense: physical blindness, a disability guaranteed to prevent what she thought might be imminent failure.

The question science has neglected to confront is: What are the fundamental operations of intellectual function that produce such reactions, and how indeed can thought processes, which are obviously involved, cause such selective change in the physical activity of the body?

Another marvelous example of quite elegant intellectual capacities in the absence of conscious awareness occurs in the sleepwalker. The sleepwalker formulates a very specific intention and recruits all his body activities to carry out the intention, usually not stopping until the act is completed or frustrated.

One of my favorite examples of the unconscious intellect is the prank some psychology students played on their professor. Learning that people could be unconsciously "conditioned," one day the students all conspired to assume postures of great interest and eagerness and attention when their professor lectured from a certain spot at the side of the classroom. When he moved from that spot, the students would slouch, whisper and otherwise looked bored. Within minutes the professor became glued to the spot where the students paid attention. To me this is not a mechanical "conditioning" as the psychologists are wont to explain, but an instance of the remarkable abilities of the unconscious intellect.

Law Twelve: We cannot directly know or experience or have any conscious awareness of the nature of our own mental processes. That is, we cannot be aware of *how* we are thinking *when* we are thinking.

Take trying to learn anything. All you know is that when you have certain bits of information and make some mental effort, you learn something. You have no idea how you accomplish the learning, i.e., you have no awareness of *how* you were learning *when* you were learning. Thinking about this puzzle, I developed a principle—modeled after the Heisenberg principle—to explain this paradox.

In quantum mechanics, the Heisenberg principle states that if you know the momentum of a particle, you can't know its exact location in space, and if you know the energy of a particle, you can't know its exact location in time.

Because I often find science very amusing, I devised the Brownenberg principle which says that if you are busy processing information in your brain, you can't know you are processing information because the information being processed is occupying the same neuronal space that is needed to become aware of what is being processed.

And of course, conversely, if you are aware of information that *has been* processed, you can't be processing new information at that moment of awareness because the mechanisms for awareness occupy the same neuronal space needed to process new information.

In summary, it is on the basis of these laws that I conclude human beings possess capacities of mind that are literally beyond genius.

Until this present decade there have been many prohibitions, both scientific and philosophic, against exploring the reality of the nonphysical mind. But today, at last, there is a multitude of signs that at least part of the extraordinary and untapped human potential is emerging to be recognized and used. We cannot project the future for the coming Age of Mind, for, as I wrote elsewhere, "the new horizons of mind revealed to an expanded awareness will be known only when awareness takes us there."

ASHLEY MONTAGU

Ashley Montagu spent his teenage years prowling about England's Royal Museum, pouncing upon its specimens and making it clear that physical anthropology was his passion. It was an early passion: At twelve Montagu was reading books on neurology and anatomy, and by the age of fourteen he was into skull collecting. One of the skulls he came upon was so unusual that he took it to the eminent Sir Arthur Keith of the Royal College Museum for identification. Sir Arthur congratulated the young scientist for having discovered an ancient skull, typically found only along the Thames River.

This early precocity led directly into London's University College for advanced studies in physical anthropology. The intense, early fascination with the human body and its history begat a writing career of over sixty books, moving out from such central subjects as physiology and anatomy to the broader realms of psychology, race, evolution and heredity, love, aggression, touching, human development, sexuality and the history of science.

Such an adventurous spirit was not to be contained in one place: By 1927, Montagu had emigrated to the United States, where he became a research scholar with the American Museum of Natural History. Later, he spent some seven years teaching anatomy at

N. Y. U. Medical School, followed by eleven years at the Hahneman Medical College in Philadelphia.

His prodigious career as an author occurred somewhat fortuitously when Rutgers University hired him to found an anthropology department, only to come up so short on funds that there was salary money for neither chairman nor department. Suddenly, Montagu found himself lecturing and writing, and he has not stopped since.

Escape from the academic life is frequently an escape from the physical attrition that usually accompanies the lifelong academician. In Montagu's case, the escape was spectacular. Now in his seventies, Montagu not only looks twenty years younger, but also talks, thinks and moves like a man much younger. Still, as he sees it, growing young is an innate human ability which few humans either understand or take advantage of.

Ashley Montagu believes that specific to the human species, there is a trait that he terms "neoteny," a Greek construction meaning "stretched-out newness" or "prolonged youth." This refers to the well-known fact that in simians and, particularly, humans the period of infancy is immensely drawn out. This is to say that humans are not, like lower species, genetically programmed to become fixed adults after a too brief childhood; humans have a protracted period of free time to learn and acquire gradually the information and skills they need for their lives.

The importance of human neoteny is that humans do not have to "age" or become fixed into "adulthood," with its stereotyped roles of appearance or behavior. Humans do not have to grow old—they just believe they do. Here Montagu touches on a somatic theme, that different attitudes and forms of behavior are functions which can control the physiological structure of the human:

> By far the most important part of extending neotenine development is in our behavior and our attitudes. If a person is spiritually young, he will do better in physical health and in physical develop-

ment and won't age as rapidly as people who are already moribund spiritually. Those who retain this inner light will keep the qualities of youthfulness to the last moment of their lives. This is what keeps a human being alive—otherwise, he dies, no matter how physically well he may be.

When not lecturing or writing, Ashley Montagu gardens around his house in Princeton, New Jersey. Also, each day he dances—with a partner if there is one available or without a partner if there is none.

In his multifaceted manner, Montagu has addressed the human condition with a rare combination of wit, passion and clarity, and he does so with an eloquence that has made him one of the most widely read and heard anthropologists of the twentieth century. The bibliography below contains a mere suggestion of his many-sided writings.

BIBLIOGRAPHY

1._____.*Man's Most Dangerous Myth: The Fallacy of Race*, 1942.
2._____.*On Being Human*, 1950.
3._____.*The Natural Superiority of Women*, 1953.
4._____.*Touch: The Human Significance of the Skin* 1971.
5._____.*The Nature of Human Aggression*, 1976.

My Conception of the Nature of Human Nature

ASHLEY MONTAGU

MY conception of human nature has developed over a period of fifty years. It has entailed the study of many different fields. It has been a very exciting exploration which has led me into the most unexpected places and to unanticipated interests and conclusions.

In the course of my studies I found myself entering into territories that had hitherto been inadequately explored or not explored at all. I found myself often startled by the stereotypy and formalism with which "authorities" repeated the errors of their predecessors, in such matters as race and in committing all sorts of pseudological rationalizations based on arbitrary definitions which were generally accepted as axiomatic. I found that such terms as "savage," "primitive," "advanced," "higher," "lower," "human nature," "instinct," "constitution," "heredity," "atavism," "puberty," "embryo," "fetus," "disease," and many others constituted lamentable examples of the systematics of confusion. As Goethe put it so aptly in *Faust:*

> For just where fails the comprehension,
> A word steps promptly in as deputy.
> With words 't is excellent disputing;
> Systems to words 't is easy suiting.*

In short, where a clear idea was wanting, a word could always be found to take its place. So from an early period in the development of my studies I decided to abandon all definitions until a knowledge of the way things really operated made definitions possible. In this I was greatly helped by reading Percy Bridgman's *The Logic of Modern Physics* (1927), and many conversations I had with that delightful man. Definitions, surely, cannot be meaningful at the beginning of an inquiry; they can only become so, if at all, at the end of one.

It was as a consequence of my being able to integrate a vast amount of knowledge drawn from every science that could possibly have anything to contribute toward the better understanding of the nature of human nature, and from innumerable observations based on the everyday lives of different peoples, as well as from premeditated and unpremeditated experiment, on humans and other animals, that what I consider to be both a scientifically and humanistically validatable view of human nature emerged.

I see the origin of human nature at the very beginning of life itself, I see it in the process of reproduction at the most primi-

---

* Johann Wolfgang Von Goethe, *Faust,* trans. Bayard Taylor (London Strahan & Co., 1871), pt. 1, sc. 4.

> Denn eben wo Begriffe fehlen,
> da Stellt ein Wort zu rechten Zeit sich ein.
> Mit Worten lässt sich trefflich streiten
> mit Worten ein System bereiten.

tive cellular level, as when a single cell divides into two. Having observed such cell division in an amoeba, for example, one can perform a simple experiment which is very enlightening. If one removes one amoeba from the other by placing it on the undersurface of a slide, it will be observed that each amoeba immediately begins to move toward the other, a phenomenon which has been called *prototaxis*. Prototaxis appears to be a universal phenomenon, from the single-celled to the mul-ticelled organism.

In short, I see the need—or drive, or urge—of organisms to be with one another as originating in the reproductive process itself. It is not only that every cell originates from another cell but also that every cell has for some time been part of another cell.

The cells of every functioning organism must cooperate with one another. It is when this cooperation is interfered with or threatened in some way that the organism begins to malfunc-tion and to have its very existence imperiled.

The directiveness which characterizes the functioning of all organisms at both the organic, or physiological, and behavioral levels is toward cooperation. And as I see it, cooperation has been the most important factor in the evolution of living crea-tures. And, to make a big quantum leap, of no creature is this more true than it is of the human.

To understand the nature of human nature it is necessary to understand the unique evolutionary history of humanity.

Humans are mammals who belong to the order of Primates. The Primates, consisting of the lemurs, loris, monkeys, apes and all forms of humans, living and extinct, are—with the exception of humans and baboons—all forest or woodland dwellers. Animals that live in forests are predominantly plant eaters, vegetarians. Most, if not all, primates will eat insects, birds' eggs, snails and lizards. Baboons will occasionally eat small antelopes, chimpanzees will occasionally eat juvenile baboons, but humans alone are omnivorous. And that fact tells us something about the manner in which our predecessors became human.

For creatures who live in forests all that one needs to do to survive is to live upon the plant foods the forest provides; the table, as it were, is laid; and there is no great challenge required to supply it. On the other hand, when what were formerly forests are transformed into savannahs with reduced vegetation, owing to changes in the rainfall of the region, only those animals are likely to survive who are able to adapt themselves to the new challenges of the environment.

It is not that our ancestors abandoned the trees, but that our ancestors were abandoned by the trees. Expelled, as it were, from their Garden of Eden, our anthropoid ancestors were faced with the necessity of enlarging their dietary. This we know at first to have included small animals, slow-moving ones, juveniles and the like. After the lapse of a considerable period of time this continuation of food gathering was extended to embrace larger game. This was achieved by the invention of a revolutionary method of supplementing food obtained by gathering—hunting.

Hunting places an immediate selective premium upon the ability to make the most appropriately successful responses to the challenges of the environment. That is the definition of intelligence. Hunting places a high selective pressure upon problem-solving activity. Animals don't run in straight lines, they zigzag all over the place. This calls for rapid decision making, the elaboration with great rapidity of changing logistics and strategies. In the course of time it is found that hunting in cooperation with others is more likely to be successful than hunting alone. Under such cooperative hunting conditions it is also discovered that communicating changes in logistics and strategies to others by sounds, upon which conventionalized meanings have been bestowed, constitutes a most efficient means of signaling. In this manner speech might have been born, or at least developed. Next to touch itself, speech to this day remains the best means of putting people in touch with one another and of reducing the distance between them. Hunting led to a variety of inventions for the capture of prey and for the treatment of their remains: hunting implements, snares, pitfalls, traps and bone and stone tools for cutting, scraping, drilling and otherwise preparing the parts of animal bodies. All this constitutes the learned part of the environment, and the learned part of the environment is culture. Such learning must be transmitted if it is to be perpetuated—and not only transmitted, but also stored. In order to store and retrieve information one must have a warehouse large enough for such purposes. Hence, the brain enlarges to accommodate the necessary changes and also, we may presume, as a result of the new uses to which it is put.

A reflection of the late increase in brain size is the fact that the greatest rate of increase in brain size occurs in the human fetus between the end of the sixth and the end of the ninth month—from a volume of 60 cubic centimeters to 350 or 400 cubic centimeters. This is a spectacular rate of growth, roughly one milligram a minute! A baby with such a large brain must be born when it normally is. For if it were not born then, its head would be unable to pass through the four inches of the birth canal, and that would be the end of the species. So the human baby is born in a highly immature condition, when it is only half gestated. The other half of its gestation is completed outside the womb, with the help of a mother who has been highly selected in the course of human evolution for her ability to minister to the dependent needs of the infant.

Gestation within the womb, uterogestation, lasts an average of 266.5 days, and so does gestation outside the womb, exterogestation, the period that terminates with the infant's first successful attempts to crawl about under his own steam. Were the baby's uterogestative period extended as every other developmental period is in the development of the individual, it would last between twenty and twenty-two months instead of nine. Indeed, the duration of the uterogestative period is the only developmental period in which the great apes and humans resemble each other. The period of infancy is especially greatly extended in humans, and the human infant remains dependent upon a caretaker for his continued growth and development much longer than any other primate.

To meet the vitally important needs of the infant, the mother has been elaborately prepared throughout pregnancy, and her ability to do so is further augmented by many further changes which she undergoes with the birth of the child. Anyone who has witnessed the birth of a child under nonmedical conditions will know that the bonding which takes place between mother and child from the moment that she first beholds the child is probably the most important event in the history of that couple. The evidence indicates that the first thirty minutes constitute the critical sensitive period in which this maternal-infant bonding occurs.

In the small populations that characterized prehistoric humans, populations which numbered between thirty and fifty individuals, the birth of a child would have been regarded as an important event. As we know from existing gatherer-hunter peoples, intensive breast-feeding extended over a period of four or more years acts as an effective contraceptive, so that children born to such women are separated by years from each other. Furthermore, infant mortality was probably comparatively high, hence the high premium placed upon mothers capable of tender loving care. Such tender, loving care is vital for the survival of the infant; without it the infant would not prosper and would die. Fathers in such prehistoric societies would be selected for their ability to minister to the needs of their families, and would be selected both by social and evolutionary pressures.

In such small prehistoric societies everyone knew everyone else intimately, and everyone was more or less involved in everyone else's welfare, for the principle that bound the members of such societies together was cooperation. An uncooperative individual threatened the existence of the group and would either be removed or forced to remove himself from the group. In other words, a very high value was placed upon cooperative behavior, so that over the course of five million years or so of human evolution, genetic constitutions favoring the predisposition to cooperative behavior were established.

Cooperative behavior, especially at the human level, is but another name for love. What the loving mother does for her infant, what the infant grows to do for his mother and others, what the father does for his wife and children, what each of the members of the small prehistoric gatherer-hunter populations did for one another, their altruism—each and every one of such behaviors is a form of love.

The human at birth is, then, the consequence of a long

evolutionary history, which orients his principal needs in the direction of growth and development as a cooperative, polymorphously educable, highly intelligent, loving creature.

Every human being is born with an inbuilt system of values. Those values are its basic needs—so called because they must be satisfied if the organism is to survive. The basic needs are the needs for oxygen, food, liquid, rest, sleep, activity, bowel and bladder elimination, and the avoidance of dangerous stimuli. These are the needs which must be satisfied if the organism is to survive physically. But if the organism is to grow and develop as a human being, a healthy human being, then the most basic of its needs for survival is the need for love. This means not merely the need to be loved, but also the need to love others. Every baby is already endowed at birth with the ability to love its mother, but it has to be loved in order to grow and develop its greater ability for love.

These statements are not theories, they are facts, based upon the observation of an immense number of cases. For example, how do we know that a newborn baby is able to love its mother? Simply by observing what it does for its mother. To illustrate: When a baby is born there may be excessive postpartum bleeding, failure of the uterus to undergo reduction, or failure to complete the third stage of labor, that is, detachment and ejection of the placenta. What the obstetrician with all his knowledge and technology cannot achieve, a newborn baby placed to suckle at his mother breast is able to achieve within ten minutes. The suckling at the breast causes messages to be sent through the spinal cord up into the hypothalamus of the brain and thence into the pineal gland, which then begins to secrete two hormones, prolactin and oxytocin. Both are important in getting the breast milk to flow freely into the baby's mouth in response to its suckling, while the oxytocin is, in addition, especially effective in producing contractions of the uterus and vasoconstriction of the uterine vessels, thus arresting the bleeding and causing the detachment and ejection of the placenta and, finally, stimulating the return of the uterus to normal size, which—by the way—it will never achieve in the absence of a suckling baby.

What this, among other things, indicates is that there resides more intelligence in the lips of one newborn baby than in all the brains of all the obstetricians and pediatricians put together. Baby and mother as a nursing couple confer innumerable benefits upon each other. The bonding which occurs between husband and wife at the birth of a baby, and as a result of such other children as they may have, further reenforces and enlarges and deepens their involvement in each other. It is at this time that we can perceive how goal directed the human infant is toward the achievement of growth and development as a loving being. For if we facilitate that growth and development by providing the necessary conditions of love and physical sustenance, then we observe the product as a healthy human being, and by a healthy human being I mean one who is able to love, to work, to play and to use his or her mind as a finely tempered instrument. We observe, on the contrary, that when a child has been failed in the need for love, whatever other qualities he may develop, he will frequently fail to grow and develop normally, both physically and mentally; and whether he does so or not, he will always be deficient in the ability to love. In brief, such a person will be deficient in the most fundamentally important humane and humanizing quality that is the indispensable condition for mental health.

Love stands like the sun in our solar system—at the center

of the system of basic needs which revolve around it like the planets round the sun. This has never been more beautifully expressed than by George Chapman (1559–1634), friend and fellow actor of Shakespeare:

> I tell thee, Love is Nature's second Sun, Causing a spring of virtues where he shines; And as without the Sun, the World's great eye, All colours, beauties both of Art and Nature, Are given in vain to men; so without Love All beauties bred in women are in vain, All virtues born in men lie buried; For Love informs them as the Sun doth colours; And as the Sun, reflecting his warm beams Against the earth, begets all fruits and flowers; So Love, fair shining in the inward man, Brings forth in him the honourable fruits Of Valour, with virtue, and haughty thoughts, Brave resolution: and divine discourse Oh, 'tis the Paradise, the heaven of earth.*

These lines tell us, among other things, that poets have a way of arriving at truths which scientists in their more pedestrian ways may take a somewhat longer time to arrive at.

The inbuilt system of values of humans clearly tells us what we *ought* to do if we would grow and develop as human beings, as healthy human beings. For it is by this time abundantly clear that when we fail children in their needs, and most importantly in the need for love, we cripple them for life in their ability to function as warm, loving, human beings. And to complement this we find that when children are satisfied in their need for love, they grow and develop into healthy human beings, who are able to love, to work, to play, even though they may not always be able to use their minds as fine instruments of precision.

---

* George Chapman, *All Fools*, act 1 sc. 1.

It should be clear, then, that the inbuilt system of biological values of humans is directed toward the growth and development of healthy human beings. In the case of humans this especially refers to mental health, for what makes humans specifically human are their behavioral capacities and abilities. And it is because humans have moved into an entirely new zone of adaptation—namely, culture, the mentally constructed and learned part of the environment, through which their principal adaptations to the environment are made—that their mental health will always remain of paramount importance in determining the success of their adaptations. That is why it is so extremely important for us to understand what the criteria of mental health are, how they came to be so firmly rooted as a consequence of the evolutionary history of humanity, and finally, how our understanding of the nature of the inbuilt system of biological values that characterizes every human bridges what philosophers have always claimed is an unbridgeable gap, namely, the so-called abyss that is supposed to separate the world of fact from the world of what ought to be. Philosophers have been unable to cross that *pons asinorum* because they were simply lacking in the knowledge necessary to negotiate it. What humanity's inbuilt system of values tells us is that if our species is to survive, then we must afford our children the opportunities to love, to work, to play and to exercise their minds.

The child is not born a *tabula rasa* upon which we inscribe our instructions for his or her development, although from our recent conduct toward children it would seem that that is how we regard them. But the truth is that the human infant is born with all its potentialities directed toward fulfillment in physical and mental health. It is the unawareness or disregard and frustration of those potentialities that leads to disoperative behavior. Such disoperative behavior, especially in children, often constitutes a desperate signal for help, for attention to their need for love. I see a great deal of aggressive behavior in humans simply as love frustrated. What such behavior calls for is love, not counteraggression.

Western society has long failed to understand the nature of the needs of infant and child, and often in its attempt to make things better, it has made them worse, as witnessed by the contemporary obstetrical approach to childbirth. Childbirth is approached, as if it were a disease or disorder, with a battery of technological devices and drugs which for the most part do more harm than good and are most unnecessary. These are applied by overtrained, overspecialized, overtechnologized persons in a dehumanizing manner in a dehumanized, antiseptic environment. Fetal monitoring; elective inductions; the administration of drugs which at the very least deprive mother and infant of normal healthy responses to the parturient experience; and now, increasingly, the delivery of babies by Caesarean section as a substitute for normal vaginal delivery (and this in disregard of all the evidence that Caesarean section has unfavorable effects on individuals delivered by that method)—all these represent a virtually complete disregard for the human requirements of what should be the most dramatically binding event in the history of a family, although there are some hospitals that are attempting to remedy this situation. The spreading home-childbirth movement is yet another evidence of the growing dissatisfaction with the dehumanizing obstetrical approach to childbirth.

My growing understanding of the importance of the childbirth experience has caused me for many years now to focus a great deal of my attention upon this fundamental period in the life of the child, the person, the family and society, for it is at this time that I see the future of every person being created—for better or for worse. Indeed, I regard our manner of dealing with the conceptus in the womb, from conception to birth, as equally important. Of course, every developmental period is important, but none are as fundamentally important as the earliest periods. It is at these early periods that we tend to do the most damage. The promise of the child is distorted and frustrated, deformed and desensitized. That is why adults have been appropriately described as deteriorated babies. And the great tragedy for most people lies in the difference between what they were capable of becoming and what they have been forced to become.

What they have, for the most part, become is not what it was in their nature to become, but what they were nurtured into becoming, a nurture based on confused, false and destructive values.

I do not subscribe to the view that humans are born neither good nor evil. I believe that the evidence unequivocally shows that humans are born with the ability to confer benefits upon their mothers, and that they behave as if they expected their mothers to confer benefits upon them. I see that when this occurs, both of them prosper, and when it does not, each of them fails. I see each of them endeavoring to develop in a reciprocally beneficial relationship, and I see this as the basic pattern of the human developmental process—in short, that our evolutionary history encoded in our genes enjoins us to live as if to live and love were one.

KARL PRIBRAM

One of the great philosophers of the seventeenth century was Gott-fried Wilhelm von Leibnitz, and one of his most powerful ideas was a theory which led to the development of a most extraordinary inven-tion: the hologram.

It was Leibnitz's idea that beneath all things material and mental were bundles of energy called monads. He believed that both material particles and mental ideas had their common roots in underlying monads of energy which, in themselves, were neither physical nor mental, neither in space nor time—rather, they were the ultimate units from which both space and time were derived.

This interesting bit of metaphysics might seem to be only another dusty corner of history except for the fact that the theory of monads, which was based on Leibnitz's own discovery of calculus, is also the theory of the hologram: namely, the theory of how that which we experience as spatial and temporal can be stored in distributed units of information that are not, themselves, specifically spatial or tempo-ral; but when refocused, the same spatial and temporal dimensions will appear again. That is what we see when we see a three-dimen-sional figure in a hologram moving and talking to us. In the hologram, objective space and time are created from information on a film that is not on a specific spot of the film surface but is distributed, like a blurred image, all over the surface.

A pool of water records the falling of many pebbles through its surface by the expanding ripples it sends out. A holographic film is like a pond with a permanent record of all the ripples caused by information dropping into it. But, surprisingly enough, human memory and perception are also like such a pond, an insight that occurred to Karl Pribram in the late 1960s, thereby making Leibnitz contemporary once more.

The holographic model seemed to Pribram the best way of explaining the peculiar nature of human memory. Brain researchers had originally thought that memories were stored in specific parts of the brain, e.g., visual memories were in the occipital lobes, or hearing memories were lodged in the temporal lobes of the brain. This turned out not to be the case: Neurosurgeons noticed that massive injuries to different sections of the brain did not, as expected, destroy the memories that were supposed to be stored there. The nature of memory in relation to the brain made no sense, inasmuch as it appeared that memories seemed to be stored everywhere in general but nowhere in particular.

The model that could best account for this curious situation was that of the hologram: It appeared that the human brain functioned in the same way as a hologram, not storing information in one place, but distributing it out of focus throughout the organism—when one remembers an event or scene, the distributed information is refocused and the information clearly recalled. Karl Pribram is a neuropsychologist, committed to understanding the relation between brain function and human consciousness, and he has suggested the hologram as a model not only for human memory but also for human perception. In the latter instance, Pribram suggests the startling idea —at least to a non-Leibnitzian—that the orderly world we see is not necessarily "out there," because brain research suggests that the human brain has a tendency to create the experience of objective order even when there is no objective order "out there." For example, from random noises certain sensory cells respond as if a single line of sound is being perceived—not merely a random jumble of sounds. Here, in Dr. Pribram's essay, will be found the same theme as in Feldenkrais's essay: that the human nervous system is genetically aggressive in imposing order on the "objective" world.

Karl Pribram (the surname is Czech) was born in Vienna in 1919, but by the time he was twenty years of age he was a naturalized American citizen and had just received his Bachelor of Science degree from the University of Chicago. He stayed at the university, where he received his medical degree in 1941. After several years practicing neurosurgery in Chicago, he began moving steadily into the research area, first with primates in the Yerkes Laboratories, then with humans in the Yale University Medical School.

In 1959 he joined the Department of Psychology and Psychiatry at Stanford University, where he continues his teaching and research.

Karl Pribram's published research is enormous for a man still in his middle years: all told, over 200 articles, books and edited books, including the famous *Languages of the Brain*, one of the landmark summaries of contemporary brain research. Dr. Pribram has published articles and edited a book with the renowned Soviet neuropsychologist A.R. Luria. Both men have been considered geniuses of twentieth-century brain research. With the recent death of Luria, Karl Pribram stands alone as the world's most eminent psychologist of neural functions.

BIBLIOGRAPHY

1._____.ed.*Brain and Behavior*, 4 vols., 1969.
2._____.ed.*The Hippocampus*, 2 vols., 1969.
3._____.*Perception and its Disorders*, 1970.
4._____.*Languages of the Brain*, 1971.
5._____.*Psychophysiology of the Frontal Lobes*, 1973.
6._____.*Freud's Project for a Scientific Psychology*, 1975.

From Infinities to No-thing: An Exploration of Brain Function

KARL PRIBRAM

ARISTOTLE defined man as the rational animal. Man's happiness, therefore, depended not only on pleasure, the fulfillment of needs, but also on the fulfillment of his rational capacities. Rationality implies the ability to analyze: The root from which the word rational is derived is also the root of ratio, divide.

In keeping with the Aristotelian view, and especially successfully since the Renaissance, Western man has cultivated his rational, analytic capabilities. He has, for the most part, developed knowledge, science, at the expense of wisdom, finding his universe filled with particulate detail which failed to provide an integrated view of the whole.

Throughout this period, philosophers have cautioned against this one-sided approach to happiness. Aristotle had not eschewed pleasure, he had stated only that pleasure was not enough if man were to be truly human. In our own century

Abraham Maslow made explicit the hierarchical nature of man's requirements for happiness: Rational fulfillment presupposes the fulfillment of more basic needs.

Meanwhile, phenomenological and existential thinkers began to point out that man-in-his-universe might not appear the same as man, the center of his universe. Jung brought an emphasis on spirituality to bear on the behavioral sciences— spirit defined in terms of infinities; universals; the collective (therefore undivided, unrational) unconscious; the instinctive, shared aspects of the human potential. And even behaviorists began to note that behavior is predicated on an interaction between man as an organism and the environment of that organism. Behaviorists opted to emphasize either organism *or* environment in this duality; but they need not have taken this reductive path, and at least some may, in the future, come more into concert with the phenomenal-existential approach.

These problems regarding part *versus* whole also come to a focus in the mind/brain issue. Over the past two centuries it has become clear that man's rationality and his mental functions in general are especially dependent on his brain. Thus, what makes man human is his brain. However, controversies have raged as to whether mental, and therefore brain, functions were all of a piece or whether they were divisible into faculties, separate processes that had to become integrated by some superordinate homunculus or executive "ego". In the neurosciences the separate-parts view reigned as the sole explanatory principle, apparently undisputable, until recently. Now there is a body of evidence to show the relevance, in at least two problem areas, of a sophisticated and precise wholistic approach. Let us look at these two areas and see what they have to offer in shaping our view of human nature.

WISDOM AND INFINITY

The brain regulates not only the body's interactions with the surrounding world but also the various bodily processes, man's basic physiological needs per se. Many of these processes, even those within the brain itself, are cyclic and rhythmic. The heart beats, peristaltic waves of gut aid digestion, sex hormones wax and wane, nerve cells spontaneously fire at periodic intervals. The regulation of these cyclicities has been familiarized under the concept "homeostasis"—the idea of a steady state achieved by a negative-feedback mechanism which turns down the production of a substance or discharge as it accumulates.

In my laboratory we have found that the part of the brain that regulates these bodily cyclicities also copes with recurring regularities in environment. For both internal and external regulations a special form of memory is invoked which monitors the substances and episodes involved. The nature of this memory (ordinarily called "episodic" or, when brief sequences are involved, "short-term" memory) has puzzled scientists for many decades. Recently, however, a physical scientist by the name of Spencer Brown (1972) faced a similar problem in engineering, provided a solution and saw the wide-ranging implications of his solution.

Spencer Brown's problem was to deal with oscillations of the wheels of a railroad train which suddenly came to a halt in a tunnel. To solve the problem of how many such oscillations had taken place (thus to identify how many wheels had actually traversed rather than oscillated across a sensor) Brown had to utilize an imaginary number ($\sqrt{-1}$) in the Boolean (binary) algebra. The reason for this was that the number of oscillations could be infinite, and thus no simple "real" solution to the problem existed.

Cyclicities are not bounded. The ordinary logic of real-number mathematics is therefore inadequate to deal with the problem. Take a line of infinite length (or a cycle of infinite length) and divide it in half. You now have two lines (or cycles) of infinite length. And you also have the *fact* that a half line (or cycle) equals the whole. Whether you want to attend to or use the half or the whole depends on circumstances, on what else is going on, the context in which use or attention is demanded. As Solomon so *wisely* judged, when there is a property dispute, dividing a roast in half may be perfectly equitable, but dividing a baby is not.

Our work has shown that the frontal lobes of the brain, that part which was once so freely severed in the procedure of leukotomy or lobotomy, is concerned in making such episode-specific, context-sensitive judgments. Wisdom, therefore, is dependent on an entirely different brain mechanism from that which allows us to accumulate knowledge. Knowledge is categorical; knowledge depends on identifying differences among a finite set of alternatives. Knowledge is comprised of information.

Wisdom, by contrast, rests on processing infinities. Paradoxes abound: Halves equal wholes when they are lines, but not when they are babies. The greater a hunger, the greater the satisfaction. The greater the hunger, the greater the disappointment. Satisfaction equals disappointment? Sometimes. The use of an imaginary number to solve such problems mathematically indicates that there are no *single* solutions in this domain. The appropriate behavior depends on the context in which the problem arises. There is no such single solution to being hungry—eating more after a Thanksgiving dinner will not take care of recurring appetite the following weekend nor stave off starving at Christmas.

In his search for knowledge man has paid little heed to understanding the roots of wisdom. I have at times voiced to my scientific colleagues some of the problems discussed in the paragraphs above, and their answer has always been either that one cannot deal at all with infinities or that one simply sets arbitrary bounds and then solves the problems in that fashion. But these answers are inadequate. There is a domain of every-day experience and behavior which depends on our deep understanding of infinities and paradoxes, and the rules of operation in this domain are very basically different from those that we ordinarily employ to acquire and use knowledge.

Not that this domain has been completely ignored. Matte Blanco in a volume entitled *The Unconscious as Infinite Sets*, published in 1975, tackles the issues involved. Gregory Bateson (1972) has faced the problems, as have his students and colleagues, especially with regard to interpersonal communication. (1967). But these are the exceptions. Formal schooling of necessity ignores wisdom, because we know so little of its formal structure. Perhaps recognizing that the problem exists can be the first step in facing it. Perhaps no more can be done than to distinguish wisdom and its base in infinities from knowledge based on rationality, i.e., division, categorizing, particularizing. Or perhaps this statement of the problem will be but a beginning.

The second area of inquiry which has yielded to a precise wholistic formulation has to do with the brain mechanisms involved in perception and memory. One of the major problems of brain function that has deterred behavioral scientists and philosophers from paying heed to the developments in the neurosciences has been the lack of any plausible model for memory storage. Lashley (1950) dramatized this problem in his statement, made less than three decades ago, that after a lifelong search for the neural substrate of memory traces he had reluctantly come to the conclusion that despite behavioral evidence to the contrary, learning was just not possible. The basis for this statement is that cutting brain pathways or even removing large pieces of brain does not remove any particular memory or set of memories. In some fashion or other the input to the brain from the senses must become distributed before it is stored.

Over the past decade the deficiency of our ability to provide a plausible model for a distributed store has been remedied. Dennis Gabor (1948) gave a precise mathematical formulation for such a store, which was subsequently implemented in the process of holography. A hologram is made on a photographic film by storing directly the waves of light reflected by or transmitted through objects without bringing them to focus by a lens. Gabor's mathematic formulations are called spread functions because they describe the spreading, or blurring, of every point of light over the surface of the film. The blur is not haphazard, however. It is composed of the waves created by each point of light, much as such waves are created by a pebble striking the placid surface of a pool. Many simultaneously striking pebbles will ruffle the water's surface in patterns of ripples, each composed of expanding wave fronts. The hologram is a frozen record of patterns of ripples. Gabor's major contribution was to show that focused images of the source of the ripple patterns could readily be reconstructed from the hologram. The technique of image reconstruction demands only the knowledge of how the blurred image was produced. In our space program such blurs occur because the photographic satellite is speeding by its target; subtracting the speed from the photo by computer provides the image. Similarly, performing the inverse transform on a hologram (by computer or optical system) will constitute a focused image from the distributed (spread) store.

It became evident that the hologram could provide the long-sought plausible model of memory storage in the brain. In addition to the distributed nature of holographic memory and the ready mechanism of image reconstruction that it made possible, holography provided additional important advantages. Larger amounts of memory could be stored than by any other technique; an associative function characterized the holographic process; and reconstructed images did not fall on the holographic film, but were projected away from it, just as we do not see images on the surface of receptors or the brain.

A caveat must be noted at this point. The holographic model is meant to handle only one aspect of brain function: the distribution of sensory input before storage and the mechanism of image construction and reconstruction. The model does not deal with categorization, with the response mechanisms of pattern recognition, especially those of identifying objects in space, or with the formation of signs and symbols. It is gratifying to have found a plausible model for distribution in memory and image reconstruction. Gratification should not lead to overgeneralizing and extending the model to areas of inquiry where the it is patently not applicable.

Initially, of course, the neural hologram was but a metaphor. Over the past decade, however, more and more evidence in support of a rigorous neural holographic model has been obtained in laboratories as distant from each other as Leningrad, Pisa and Stanford. The major contributions have been made by a group headed by Fergus Campbell and John Robson at Cambridge University (1968); Daniel Pollen at Harvard (1974); and Russell De Valois at Berkeley. (1978). What was needed was evidence that the brain operated as a frequency analyzer—an analyzer of the vibrations, the waves, that compose the frequency spectrum of physical energies. Ohm (1843) and Helmholtz (1867) had already performed experiments almost a century before to show that the ear and auditory nervous system operated as a frequency analyzer of sound. Bekesy (1967) using equations similar to Gabor's, constructed sets of mechanical vibrators to model the cochlea of the inner ear. He then showed that this mechanical model could be applied to the skin and that one could sense such stimulation as if it were at a distance, in a manner similar to that used in stereophonic high-fidelity systems to project the sound image away from the source speakers. Further, work from my own (1971) and other laboratories (Bernstein, 1967) indicated that the motor system is also organized to analyze periodic stimulation from the muscle system.

What remained to be shown was that the visual system operated in the frequency mode to analyze spatial relationships in constructing spatial images. This has now been accomplished in the laboratories noted above by impaling single cells in the visual system of the brain and showing that they do encode in this mode, by virtue of being tuned to one or another octave of spatial frequency. The ensemble of cells thus forms a microstructure which acts as a frequency filter—in short, a hologram. As Campbell has said, the current contribution is to show that the eye analyzes the spatial distribution of light much as the ear analyzes the temporal distribution of sound.

Thus, evidence has accumulated to show that one operation the brain performs is to resonate to the periodicities and vibrations in the energy spectrum of the environment. Images of objects are then constructed and reconstructed from the store (probably protein) based on this distributed resonating filter— the neural hologram.

This development of our understanding of brain function mirrors that encountered in quantum physics during the earlier part of the century. In studying the microstructure of the fabric of the material universe, physicists were faced with smaller and smaller units, particles which behaved more and more oddly. In fact, in some situations the description of their behavior made "them" appear to be waves rather than particles. Finally, within the nucleus of atoms particles are only temporarily constituted when energy patterns, wave forms, interact in certain ways. At least one eminent physicist, David Bohm (1971; 1973), has suggested that a hologram like "implicate" order underlies the particulate material universe.

It is important to understand fully the nature of this suggestion. The finding of a nonparticulate base of the physical world does not deny substance and reality to the ordinary world of appearances. Our discovery of the fact that the world is round does not deny its local, everyday flatness for use in walking, building, etc. Our discovery of the rotation of the earth around its axis and its trajectory in space does not do violence to our everyday readiness to rest and sleep without worry that we shall be spun away from our berth. What we want to know is how the world of appearances comes to be, how it is related to these other "realities" that our science has discovered: Just how shallow is the curvature of the earth, how do centripetal gravitational forces work, how are particles formed from hologram like flows of energy?

But another aspect of these discoveries and their interpretation, with regard both to the microstructure of the brain and to quantum and nuclear physics, is the primacy of the distributed, extended domain over the particulate. Or if not primacy, certainly complementarity exists between the two domains. In either case there is a very basic level of organization in brain and universe in which "things," as such, do not exist. Things are space bound and time bound. In the holographic frequency domain such bounds do not exist.

This, then, is a domain of no-thingness. No-thingness is not a void. The holographic universe is packed with energy, but particles, things, must be derived in order to constitute the ordinary and complementary universe of appearance. Whether derivation occurs external to and independent of sense organs and brain is at this reading difficult to gauge. As Wigner (1969), another eminent physicist, has pointed out, modern microphysics rests on establishing relationships between observations, not between observables. This is due to the fact that changes in observational technique change the observations in non-trivial ways (the Heisenberg principle).

Thus, experimental studies of both organism and environment have unveiled a wholistic, non-divided universe in which

no-thing can be located, because everything becomes distributed and extended in time and space.

Infinity and no-thing! What strange aspects of nature have
we humans come upon. The mathematics of ∞ and ○ have
challenged thoughtful investigators for millennia. Now we find
these same characteristics not only in the physical universe but
also in our own brains. *Our* very nature must thus be formed,
in part at least, in terms of these organizations. Western man
has triumphed over the obstacles to happiness in his environment. But at the same time he has barely begun to fathom his
own nature and to form a social structure consonant with this
nature. Science, especially, has eschewed coping with the nonparticulate, with the nonobjective (i.e., anything which cannot
be understood in terms of objectifying, making objects of). Nor
has science been tolerant of observations, such as precognitions
and telepathy, which do not fit into the ordinary world of
appearances and of space-time coordinates. As we have noted,
however, the holographic frequency domain collapses time and
space into simple densities of occurrences. Perhaps those who
experience paranormal phenomena tune in on this domain.
Jung called such tuning-in "synchronicity," and Lila Gatlin
(1978) has used information-measurement mathematics to
demonstrate how synchronicities can occur. What has been
missing is a scientific base for understanding such paranormal
phenomena. Only when such a base is solidly achieved can we
evaluate their "objective" validity.

My message here is that we ought to introduce into our
educational system at least some acquaintance with the logical
paradoxes of infinities, with non-objective no-thingness, with
these forms of wholistic thinking, lest we ignore the very

depths of the nature of man. Surely, it is the nature of man to be rational, but I believe it is also his nature to attempt to experience the extended universe of no-thing and to aspire to the wisdom of the infinite.

REFERENCES

Bateson, G. In: P. Watzlawick, J. Beavin and D. Jackson, *Pragmatics of Human Communication.* New York: W.W. Norton & Co., 1967.

Bateson, G. *Steps to an Ecology of Mind: Collected Essays in Anthropology, Psychiatry, Evolution and Epistemology.* San Francisco: Chandler Publishing Co., 1972.

Bekesy, G. von. *Sensory Inhibition.* Princeton: Princeton University Press, 1967.

Bernstein, N. *The Co-ordination and Regulation of Movements.* New York: Pergamon Press, 1967.

Blanco, Ignacio Matte, *The Unconscious as Infinite Sets: An Essay in Bi-Logic.* London: Duckworth & Co., 1975.

Bohm, D. Quantum theory as an indication of a new order in physics. Part A. The development of new orders as shown through the history of physics. *Foundations of Physics, 1*(4): 359–381, 1971.

Bohm, D. Quantum theory as an indication of a new order in physics. Part B. Implicate and explicate order in physical law. *Foundations of Physics, 3*(2): 139–168, 1973.

Brown, G. Spencer, *Laws of Form,* New York: Julian Press, 1972.

Campbell, F. W. and Robson, J. G. Application of Fourier analysis to the visibility of gratings. *J. Physiol., 197:* 551–566, 1968.

De Valois, R. L., Albrecht, D. G. and Thorell, L. G. Spatial tuning of LGN and cortical cells in monkey visual system. In: H. Spekreijse (Ed.) *Spatial Contrast.* Amsterdam: Monograph Series, Royal Netherlands Academy of Sciences (1978).

Gabor, D. A new microscopic principle, *Nature, 161:* 777–778, 1948.

Helmholtz, H. von. *Handbuch der physiologischen Optik.,* 1st Ed., Leipzig: Voss, 1867.

Lashley, K. S. In search of the engram. In: Society for Experimental Biology

(Great Britain), Physiological Mechanisms in Animal Behavior. New York: Academic Press, 1950, pp. 454–482.

Ohm, G. S. Uber die definition des tones, nebst daran geknupfter theorie der sirene und ahnlicher tonbildener vorrichtungen. *Ann. Physik. Chem. 59:* 513–565, 1843.

Pollen, D. A., and Taylor, J. H. The striate cortex and the spatial analysis of visual space. In: *The Neurosciences Study Program, Vol. III*, Cambridge, Mass.: The MIT Press, 1974, pp. 239–247.

Pribram, K. H. *Languages of the Brain: Experimental Paradoxes and Principles in Neuropsychology.* Englewood Cliffs, New Jersey: Prentice-Hall, 1971. (2nd Ed., Monterey, Calif: Brooks/Cole, 1977).

Wigner, E. P. Epistemology of quantum mechanics: Its appraisals and demands. In: M. Grene (Ed.) *The Anatomy of Knowledge.* London: Routledge and Kegan Paul, 1969.

CARL ROGERS

Before Carl Rogers became a psychotherapist, he was on his way to becoming a minister. And before he thought of becoming a minister, he thought he would become a farmer. Born in Oak Park, Illinois, in 1902, Rogers has the body and demeanor of a Midwestern farmer: sturdy, slow-moving and deliberate. One look and you know he is not a man to be pushed. He goes at his own pace.

That deliberate pace has threaded its way through a career that has left twentieth-century psychotherapy transformed. Rogers has been responsible for creating "client-centered therapy," and he has also been a major developer of group therapy.

Rogers obtained both the M.A. and Ph.D. degrees from Columbia University. Earlier in New York, he was for two years student at the Union Theological Seminary, then in 1927 was a fellow in psychology at the Institute for Child Guidance. From 1928 to 1930, he worked in Rochester, New York, as a psychologist for the Society for the Prevention of Cruelty to Children.

He left New York to spend five years (1940–45) as professor of psychology at Ohio State. Then, from 1945 to 1957, he was at the University of Chicago, where the counseling center became the proving grounds for client-centered therapy. Later, from 1957 to 1963, Rogers was at the University of Wisconsin at Madison, before mov-

ing to the West Coast to assume his present position as resident
fellow of the Center for the Study of the Person at La Jolla, California.

One of the hallmarks of Carl Rogers's career has been his insistence that the psychotherapeutic client be considered as a person
rather than as a patient. In order for this to be possible, the therapist
himself must have a "positive regard" for the person with whom he
is working. This attitude was considered necessary to the client-
centered approach, which as a non-Freudian therapy did not assume
the client to be dependent upon the therapist's manipulations, but
assumed the contrary: that the client was fully capable of analyzing
his own problems, of judging how to overcome these problems and
of acting to transcend them in a positive action of growth.

Respect for the individual and for his ability to be responsible for
himself is a major theme in somatic science, and Rogers, as a leading
figure in the somatic tradition, also stresses another theme: namely,
that the client—like all humans—is a being in process. This was a
revolutionary doctrine, for it took away the authoritarian power of the
psychotherapist (who could no longer pretend to be all-knowing and
all-powerful) and put the power of healing into the hands of the
person. It is easy to appreciate how Rogers's viewpoint was, for a very
long while, vigorously resisted by the psychotherapeutic profession.

Rogers felt that the therapeutic encounter should, from the beginning, establish a helpful client-therapist relationship which, in itself,
becomes the kind of healthy interpersonal relationship that the client
can extend outward into other domains of this life. This is to say that
the traditional psychoanalytic concern to establish a "transference"
of authority from patient to doctor was consciously avoided. From
Rogers's point of view, it is the form of the client-therapist relationship that determines whether the client will emerge more autonomous in behavior and judgment.

Client-Centered Therapy: Its Current Practice, Implications and

Theory was published in 1951, and its readership has grown exponentially during the past twenty-five years. But the success of client-centered therapy with single clients was only a first step in Rogers's rethinking of psychotherapy: He then moved into the area of group therapy, studying the dynamics of this more complex process. Rogers proposed a hypothetical Law of Interpersonal Relationships, which assumes that if two persons are willing to be in contact with one another and communicate with one another over an extended period of time, then the greater the congruence of understanding and communication on the part of one person, the greater the resulting congruence in communication and understanding on the part of both parties.

More than a decade of research on group process has confirmed Rogers in his expectations, and he has taken these results and elevated them to a higher sphere of application: the complex sphere of political conflict. In recent years, Rogers has agreed to work in groups where intense disagreements prevailed. In one instance it was a group of Irish Catholics and Protestants near Belfast, and in the other instance, a mock European parliament meeting in Spain. In both cases, Rogers discovered that differences which seemed unbridgeable became surmounted within the controlled process of democratic communication. This is an area Rogers is still exploring with a justified enthusiasm.

Carl Rogers sees the route of his own career as that of an amoeba: moving slowly and curiously toward any area that could provide nutrition—finding it in some cases and not finding it in others—but overall, moving from one thing to another with tolerance and openness and never with a dogmatic certainty. The essay that follows is a clear example of that irrepressible openness.

BIBLIOGRAPHY

1————.*Measuring Personality Adjustment in Children Nine to Thirteen Years of Age,* 1931.

2————.*Counseling and Psychotherapy,* 1942.

3————.*Client-centered Therapy* 1951.

4————.*On Becoming a Person,* 1961.

5————.*Freedom to Learn,* 1969.

6————.*Carl Rogers on Encounter Groups,* 1970.

7————.Rogers, Carl *Becoming Partners,* 1972.

8————.*Carl Rogers on Personal Power, 1977.*

Some New Directions: A Personal View

CARL ROGERS

I AM one of those who see our Western culture as having reached its culmination, as now approaching its death and, hopefully, its rebirth into something new and strange to us. I am far from being alone in such a perception. In a remarkable article, Jean Houston (1978) sees us as "a world that no longer works, whose lease has run out, whose paradigms are eroding."* Historian Stavrianos (1976) gives a great deal of evidence which indicates that we are approaching a new Dark Age, but one full of promise for the future. Robert Heilbronner (Campbell, 1975), economic historian, says that there is "a feeling in the pit of the stomach that great troubles and changes loom for the future of civilization as we know it. A feeling that the world is coming apart at the seams."† Willis Harman (1977) of the Stanford Research Institute reports an analysis made by him and his staff. He points to the insoluble

* Jean Houston, "Re-seeding America: the American Psyche as a Garden of Delights," *Journal of Humanistic Psychology*, 18 (winter 1978):

† From interview by Colin Campbell, "Coming Apart at the Seams," *Psychology Today*, 8 (February 1975):

problems of our civilization. The most pressing of these are caused not by the failures of our society, but by its successes. The old formulas for progress—make things bigger and faster, produce more, make more profits, use labor-saving machines—are only making things worse.

Like these others, I have come to believe that our culture is deteriorating and approaching collapse. Will it be through a nuclear holocaust? Perhaps. Possibly even more likely is what one writer calls the "destructuring of civilization," in which our institutions will gradually fall apart from their own complexity and unbearable bureaucratic weight.

But if our culture is deteriorating, what about humankind? What about communities? What about the individual man and woman? I believe that through a multitude of experiences during the past decade I am learning how we as creatures may survive the deterioration. I believe I am seeing exciting evidence of new characteristics, some of which involve a fresh perspective on the evolving possibilities of individuals, groups and communities. I think I am gaining a new vision of some of the developments in the human species which may enable it to live through the period of decay. Perhaps we are witnessing a period of expanding abilities in humankind.

What characteristics might make it possible for us to transcend this turbulent future? Drawing on the informed judgment and opinions of others, as well as my own experience and convictions, I will describe several of them.

It seems necessary to develop cooperative small communities, in place of our competitive large cities.

In these groupings we need participative modes of decision making in which the needs of all are recognized and taken into account, not simply the wishes of those in control or of a majority.

The basis for values will need to be recognized as discoverable within, rather than in dogmas or in the material world.

The rich resources of the inner world need to be explored and utilized. Inner space may be even more important than outer space, and perhaps we can learn to live an important part of our lives in it.

Experts agree that if we are to survive, drastic changes are needed in our purposes, our values and our behavior. I believe the characteristics I have mentioned may help us to transcend our present culture. But can they be achieved? I should like to tell you of some of my relevant learnings which lead me to believe they can be achieved.

Years ago I discovered some of the definable qualities of a growth-promoting climate for the individual. I found that if I could provide certain psychological attitudes, individuals in therapy could be trusted to experience their conflicts, their fears, their angers, and anxiously begin to risk becoming more mature, more inwardly harmonious persons. They made progress in becoming more openly their own experience and were thus freer and more creative.

Then I learned that these same conditions appeared to facilitate a striking process of change in intensive groups of ten or twelve, meeting for from three days to two weeks. If I could be quite fully myself with these groups, if I could deeply understand the feelings and personal meanings expressed, if above all I trusted them and prized them, a definite process was set in motion. This process ended in both individual and group gain. Individuals came to understand better their own dynamics and the ways, both useful and destructive, they were relating to others. They developed a sense of their own power. The group became a very close community, with its members often expressing surprise that they felt closer to each other than to their friends or family.

There is a body of steadily mounting research evidence, from studies carried on both here and abroad, which supports the view that when these conditions are present, changes in personality and behavior do indeed occur. Such changes have been measured in individual therapy, in groups, in classes where teachers possess facilitative attitudes and in other situations. It can be said that we know, with tentative assurance, the characteristics of the climate which promotes psychological growth.

But then we (I and other staff members) began to be more bold. Could a similar sense of community develop in a group of sixty or more? Our first attempt came close to failure, primarily because we had not been sufficiently sensitive to some of the strong negative emotions which were present. Yet it was, on the whole, encouraging.

Since then we have tried, in a variety of settings, with groups from one hundred to over two hundred, to trust the group deeply and to gently facilitate the building of close community and the concomitant development of personal insights and inner strength. Last year in Brazil we became not merely bold, but foolhardy, and took the gamble of seeing whether the same kind of process could emerge in twelve hours spent with very large groups of six hundred to eight hundred. The experience was more successful than we had dared to hope. Follow-up evidence shows many profound changes in behavior.

A few months ago a combined European and American staff met for ten days with an intercultural workshop in Spain. There were 170 members from twenty-two different nations, representing an even larger number of cultures—such as a Malaysian man who is a citizen of Denmark. Every statement had to be translated—English and Spanish being the two languages. And when French or Italian or German or Dutch was spoken, the statements had to be translated into both English and Spanish! To complicate matters further, there were politically passionate Marxists, as well as economic conservatives. There was a general dislike of the United States and its economic imperialism. Sometimes the obstacles seemed completely insurmountable. Yet in the presence of the same facilitative climate, the large group became, in every sense, a harmonious community. Not a community whose views were all similar—most assuredly not! But a community where individuals with their diverse views and convictions came to be understood and where persons and their differences were prized and respected. Individuals felt empowered to take more risks in developing themselves, in carrying through constructive social actions.

All these learnings add up to the fact that we have important skills in building cooperative communities. In these communities a patient decision-making process emerges in which every need and desire is considered and taken into account, so that no one feels left out. These decisions are beautifully crafted to take care of each person. Furthermore, the individual becomes increasingly free of values imposed by family or church or state and chooses those behaviors which are *experienced* as valuable, not those which are *said* to be valuable.

When I read that the nine European Common Market nations are soon to elect a European parliament of some four hundred members, I grow excited by the possibilities. It is reported that its function will be more symbolic than legislative. This opens still more opportunities, since they will not be rigidly bound to "party lines," but can be persons. I have little doubt that a competent international facilitative staff could initiate in this diverse international congress the same sort of process I have been describing in the Spanish workshop. Imagine such an international group reaching the point where its members could truly hear and understand and respect each other, where a cooperative sense of community developed, where humanness had a higher priority than power. The results could have the most profound significance. I do not mean that all problems would be resolved. Not at all. But even the most difficult tensions and demands become more soluble in a human climate of understanding and mutual respect. Is the world ready to try it? I doubt it.

I have little or no confidence that the skills of a facilitative international staff will be called upon, but we do have the experience and the knowledge which show that it is possible. I am also convinced that it would increase the chances of survival for all of us.

But how does this group process come about? What are the dynamics which set it in motion? Here the function of the staff is very important. Formerly we did a great deal of planning, formulating options from which the group might choose. Gradually we have learned that the most important thing we can do in preparing for such a workshop is to share ourselves openly with each other, learning to trust each other and, especially, to trust our differences. Then we can *be persons* in the group, thus giving members freedom to do the same. If at a given moment in the community one staff member is openly anxious and another is hopeful and expectant, if one is loving and another is angry and critical, the members discover that all of these feelings are acceptable and can be expressed. Thus they become more deeply persons themselves.

We listen with understanding and respect to every person. We are especially attentive to the hesitant voices, to those statements which are unpopular or unacceptable. We make it clear that there is room for every type of attitude and that all such feelings are understood and accepted. Thus each member is validated as a person.

It is also increasingly clear to us that we have little interest in *outcome*. We do not set goals. We are invested in facilitating a certain process over which we have no fundamental control. Our experience shows us that we can trust this unknown outcome to be constructive.

This process has led us into totally unexpected learnings which point in strange directions. In these groups we become one organ of a living, moving system. We have all become more intuitive, knowing without "knowing." Some have developed to a degree which can only be called psychic. They can sense, physically, when there is unexpressed anger in the group, for example. Others are very sensitive to unspoken attitudes or trends in the group. Perhaps our more primitive capability, our largely unused right brain, is beginning to function again as it so often does in less "civilized" societies. Perhaps this "metaphoric mind" can come to know a universe which is nonlinear, in which the terms time and space come to have very different meanings.

Possibly this is one of the reasons that some of our group have gone even further into the definitely paranormal world. Here I will limit myself to my own observations and experience. I have no explanation for what I shall describe. I simply know that I have observed at firsthand, and experienced myself, phenomena which I cannot explain on a rational basis or in terms of any known scientific laws. A few years ago I would have scoffed at the possibility of any such phenomena, but I cannot deny the evidence of my senses.

I would also stress that the people involved are not professional soothsayers, fortunetellers or mediums. I am speaking of honest individuals who have often been frightened by their initial paranormal experiences, but have come to regard their unusual abilities as a special gift entrusted to them. They resolutely refuse any sort of payment. I have come to know such individuals in this country and in Brazil, where a belief in the spirit world and in paranormal capacities is a deep-seated part of the culture.

I have observed incidents, among friends of mine, of what can only be described as telepathic communication. This makes me ready to believe the scientist John Lilly (1973), who tells of his experiences in such communication of ideas and feelings with a close friend, communication which came about quite unexpectedly.

I have had some experience with clairvoyance. A person I know well "saw" a close relative dying in a hospital bed in another country. A long distance call confirmed this as a fact. A woman told me of seeing her twin sister in an auto accident on a certain highway. She phoned the state police, describing the car, the person, the approximate location. The officer was greatly puzzled by her call, because they had only just received the report of the accident, which was exactly as she described.

How can we account for these experiences and many others like them which have been reported? Are there unknown waves in the atmosphere, through which visual and psychological messages can be sent and received? I do not know.

Even more mysterious is precognition. A person whom I know very well, who has received a variety of significant messages through the much-scorned Ouija board, received a message that a tragic event would occur on a specific date and that a certain family member, John, needed help. A phone call showed that John was doing very well and in no need of help. But two days after the date specified, one member of her family was killed in an auto accident. John was also near death from injuries and was indeed in need of both physical and psychological help. By what possible reasoning can such events be explained?

I have not much interest in poltergeists, the "spirits" who harass individuals or families, but a psychic research group in Brazil has assembled massive evidence in many such cases. Witnesses are interviewed separately, and every precaution is taken to preserve objectivity. The evidence appears overwhelming that some type of unknown forces or entities is able to move objects, set fires, cause disturbances, make loud sounds, and the like.

With mediums in this country and in Brazil, I have supposedly been in contact with "a spirit world." One experience will suffice. I was present at a session with a medium who works in a brightly lighted room. A small table taps out letters on the floor. There was no possibility of fraud. Toward the end of the session she asked the three of us present to concentrate on someone close to us who was deceased. In a moment the table tipped strongly toward one woman. She asked that if this was a spirit to please identify itself. The table spelled out correctly the name of her deceased sister—the person she had concentrated on. "Can you give the name of our brother?" was the next question. The table tapped correctly the name of their brother, also deceased. There were then other very significant messages, but not of a nature which could be checked. The medium knew only the first names of the persons present and could not conceivably have known the family of the woman involved. The experience was extremely convincing.

I have also been forced to consider the possibility of reincarnation, which in the past I have thought a ridiculous belief. I have seen three persons regressed to "previous lives" through hypnosis, and the changes in personality, behavior and sex seemed very believable, but nothing was given which could be validated. However, I now find more plausible the hypnotic sessions with Taylor Caldwell,* which she tended to dismiss, but which in total carry considerable conviction. But I have seen no fully verified evidence.

I have done a good deal of reading about other paranormal phenomena: psychokinesis, the ability to move or alter the shape or behavior of objects by some sort of inner energy; "out of the body" experiences; psychic healing and psychic surgery; but I have chosen to limit myself to those phenomena with which I have had trustworthy experience myself. I am well aware that others have explored much further than I.

I do not know how this world of the paranormal may change us. But I believe we are perhaps opening up vast new fields of knowledge and power—a quantum leap. And every time new forces or energies have been discovered in our universe, they have changed our perception of reality and have opened new doors and new opportunities for the human being. It seems possible that this is in process of occurring again.

---

* Jean Stearn, *The Search for a Soul: Taylor Caldwell's Psychic Lives* (New York: Doubleday & Co., 1973).

Contrary to the belief of many, this expanding discovery of the psychic world is in no way antiscientific.

In physics, the most basic of sciences, creative discoveries are taking us closer and closer to a mystic view of life, to a recognition that the more we know, the nearer our thinking is akin to that of ancient sages. A book such as Fritjof Capra's *The Tao of Physics* (Boulder, Colo.: Shambala Publications, 1975) would have been ridiculed even a generation ago. Now it can be shown that modern-day theoretical physics involves a similarity to mysticism; has a place for an overarching spiritual force, a unified cosmic energy; is not unlike the "Way" of Lao-tse and others.

Philip Slater, in his important recent book, *The Wayward Gate: Science and the Supernatural* (Boston: Beacon Press, 1977), shows how science deals with phenomena which lie outside its current system of thought. Only slowly does the scientist come to regard the evidence as "real" and thus subject to scientific investigation. The same slow process is taking place in regard to psychic phenomena.

Itzhak Bentof goes even further. Like Capra, he recognizes that in modern physics physical matter, the more deeply it is understood, is a void permeated by oscillating fields. Building on such scientific knowledge, he constructs a speculative but provocative theory which explains all psychic phenomena, and even reincarnation, in terms of already known scientific facts. Whether one agrees or not, he opens the door to many possibilities.

So what do I conclude from my own personal learnings and from the efforts of others to explain even the most improbable of these phenomena? Here I am deeply perplexed and uncertain. I have more questions than conclusions. Is the human species evolving in new ways more suitable for transcending our present culture? Perhaps. There seems to be some meaning to the development of our greater self-awareness; to the realization of our potential strength and power; to our ability to form close and harmonious communities; to our recognition that the peak of scientific knowledge is similar to the peak of mysticism; to our expansion into alternate states of consciousness; to our new tendency to develop our intuitive abilities; to our increasing acquaintance with the whole psychic realm; to our growing use of psychic forces and energy.

Perhaps, as a friend of mine has suggested, we are entering a transitional stage of evolution similar to that of the first sea creatures who laboriously dragged themselves out of the swampy bogs to begin the difficult and complex task of coping with the problems of living on land. Are we, too, evolving into new spaces? Will we discover new energies, new forces, new ways of being? Are we entering new worlds of psychic space, as well as the world of outer space? What is the future of the human spirit? To me these are tantalizing, but definitely hopeful, questions.

REFERENCES

Bentof, Itzhak. *Stalking the Wild Pendulum: On the Mechanics of Consciousness.* New York: E. P. Dutton, 1977.

Campbell, Colin. Interview with Robert Heilbronner, "Coming apart at the seams," *Psychology Today,* Vol. 8, #9, Feb., 1975, p. 95 ff.

Capra, Fritjof. *The Tao of Physics: An Exploration of the Parallels Between Modern Physics and Eastern Mysticism.* Boulder, Colorado: Shambala Publications, 1975.

Harman, W. W. The coming transfiguration, *The Futurist, Vol. XI,* #2, Feb. & April, 1977.

Houston, Jean. Re-seeding America: The American psyche as a garden of delights, *J. of Humanistic Psychology, Vol. 18,* #1, Winter, 1978.

Lilly, J. C. *The Center of the Cyclone.* New York: Bantam Books, 1973.

Slater, Philip. *The Wayward Gate: Science and the Supernatural.* Boston: Beacon Press, 1977.

Stavrianos, L. S. *The Promise of the Coming Dark Age.* San Francisco: W. H. Freeman and Co., 1976.

Stearn, Jess. *The Search for a Soul: Taylor Caldwell's Psychic Lives.* New York: Doubleday & Co., 1973. (Also a Fawcett Crest paperback.)

MARGARET MEAD

Because of the unusual nature of her family life, Margaret Mead feels that she "was brought up in my own culture two generations ahead of my time." That is quite a head start, and it indicates not only that Margaret Mead did not find her generation until the 1960s, but also makes clear that for two generations she was at odds with her own culture.

So in 1925 when a twenty-three-year-old American girl set off for Samoa for her first field study, it was most unusual: Girls of that age did not, at that time, travel far off to live for years in primitive cultures. But a twenty-three-year-old Margaret Mead did this—for her it was the most obvious and inevitable of things. Mead was reared in a household of socially concerned and intellectually vigorous parents, and they were parents who treated their firstborn in a way that was unusual in those days: She was treated as a responsible person.

Becoming an anthropologist was, indeed, the most natural thing in the world for Mead. From childhood onward her parents had inculcated in her the very attitudes and interests that are necessary for a cultural anthropologist: "For me, being brought up to become a woman who could live responsibly in the contemporary world and learning to become an anthropologist, conscious of the culture in which I lived, were almost the same thing."

Anthropology was not so much a profession as it was a vocation for Mead: reflecting her parents' own sentiments, she saw her career in anthropology as a way toward bettering humankind. During an immensely rich career, Margaret Mead became the kind of anthropologist whose work is intended for the betterment of others. She was a cultural anthropologist who interpreted to us, in a professional manner, not only other cultures but also our own culture. Margaret Mead used the critical and analytical judgment she developed over long, direct study of the peoples of seven different South Sea cultures and applied this judgment to our own culture.

Because of being an exception to her culture and because of her continued absorption in the learning of other cultures, she was an expert—and a courageous one—in interpreting to Americans what their recent cultural changes have looked like. For example, among America's leading social and behavioral scientists, she was almost alone in heralding the demand for freedom and self-determination during the 1960s as an upward turn for our culture.

Dr. Mead was centrally involved in the development of cultural anthropology during the course of this century. It is a branch of study which sees the enormous differences between human nations and peoples as differences created by different cultures. Human beings of different societies behave differently because they have *learned* to do so. They have learned from their inherited culture in such an exact way that it is as if their behavior were genetically programed.

There was one area of acculturated behavior that had never been brought into focus by science: nonverbal movement patterns that are culturally typical, such as the way a mother plays with her baby. One of the lasting contributions that she and Gregory Bateson—her former husband—made to anthropology was their insistence on the use of the camera as a scientific tool for the study of the learned movement patterns of a culture. Mead saw that beneath the verbal, imagistic lives of humans there was a silent world of movements—of raised eyebrows, of stifled smiles, of shrugged shoulders—that are as characteristic of a culture as any other feature. The camera was a ready-made tool for science to study the body of humankind, and not simply the mind.

To establish cultural anthropology as a science has involved a rigorous demonstration of just this point: that differences between urban and Stone Age behavior, or between races, are due not to genes, but to learning—"There, but for the grace of culture, go I!" This is to say that cultural anthropology is a science which undermines all forms of racism and which affirms the unity of the human race. This is also to say that a cultural anthropologist is a scientist whose pronouncements are automatically political. Margaret Mead was always fully aware of the controversial nature of her profession, and did not avoid the confrontations that frequently came her way. It would be an understatement to say that she didn't mince words: Indeed, she was fearless in stating exactly what she thought, as her essay clearly demonstrates.

The flat and unadorned honesty of Margaret Mead has, after a half century of controversial public life, emerged as one of the most admired phenomena in American life. Even though she was in advance of their culture, older Americans admired her because of her brilliance and honesty. And the younger Americans respected her because she understood their situation. In a nation where universally admired and trusted persons are almost nonexistent, Margaret Mead was held in unique respect.

That respect was shared by her fellow scientists, who elected her president of the American Association for the Advancement of Science in 1975.

BIBLIOGRAPHY

1_____..*Coming of Age in Samoa*, 1928.
2_____.*Growing Up in New Guinea*, 1930.

3_____. *The Changing Culture of an Indian Tribe*, 1932.
4_____. *Sex and Temperament in Three Primitive Societies*, 1935.
5_____. Bateson, Gregory. *Balinese Character: A Photographic Analysis*, 1942.
6_____. *Male and Female*, 1949.
7_____. Macgregor, Frances C. *Growth and Culture: A Photographic Study of Balinese Childhood*, 1951.
8_____. *Culture and Commitment*, 1970.
9_____. *Blackberry Winter: My Earlier Years*, 1972.

The Transforming Power of Culture

MARGARET MEAD

I WANT to talk about my view of human nature and what I have been able to learn during the last fifty years as I have worked back and forth between different peoples who lived as our ancestors lived many, many thousands of years ago, and then back to us and then back again to them. In this way I have learned about the strength of culture and also about the possibilities of culture change as I have worked with a people—the Manus of the Admiralty Islands—who in one generation skipped the equivalent of ten or twenty thousand years, not because their genes changed, but simply because they had put at their disposal the accumulated wisdom and skills that have been built up in the course of building our contemporary civilization.

I am particularly interested, at present, in taking the new knowledge of genetics obtained through our extraordinary new electronic equipment and in matching this new knowledge with our understanding of human cultures. This, in turn, can help us to understand that an individual with the gifts of an

Einstein could have been born among the Pygmies of the Ituri Forest in central Africa or among a people in the heart of New Guinea. With a brain as good as Einstein's, such a man might have taken an extraordinary step within a primitive society in making the suggestion that people count by tens instead of, for example, by fours, as one of my peoples did. They used to count "one, two, two-and-one, one-dog." Taking a four-legged animal as their base, they got to "dog-dog," which was 16, and then they gave up. Although the effort such a gifted individual would have had to make may seem very small to us, the step taken may be as great or greater than that taken by Einstein in making his own momentous discovery.

Fortunately, I have been in a better position to appreciate this than most people, because I have worked with a people—the Mountain Arapesh of New Guinea—who could not count beyond twenty and whose heads ached when you asked them to think logically for more than five minutes, but whose children, in the next generation, have graduated from universities and have at their disposal the accumulated scientific knowledge available to our students.

About 40 years ago it was found that if rats were placed in cages and were fed a carbohydrate diet and then were also given pure minerals and vitamins from which to make their own selection, the rats were able to select an adequate diet. The astonishing thing is that up to that time no one had known how to prepare purified vitamins and minerals in a form that allowed rats—or any living creature—to make such selections. Yet the *capacity* to make such selections goes back to plants, which are able to select nutrients from the soil; unlike plants, animals and human beings have not been able to use the same capacity. Some large animals do seek salt, but that is about all we knew about the process until the present century, during which we have worked out techniques of synthesizing vitamins and of purifying minerals. This has now allowed us to discover and utilize a capacity that has been latent and unused for an incredible length of time.

We also know now that the human infant at birth can move about 18 inches toward the head of a human being if it is placed on the body. Human infants have not had to make use of that capacity, because mothers have hands and can lift up their newborn infants. Nevertheless, the capacity exists and undoubtedly far predates in time the emergence of our species.

Exploration of the mysteries of DNA has also revealed to us that the DNA of recognition of the self and recognition of the non-self is so extremely ancient that it occurs throughout the living world, from bacteria to human beings. Our greater knowledge has made it apparent that the human being is a mosaic of genetic materials that represent the whole history of evolution, not merely human evolution but the evolution of life itself. And as different cultures have been elaborated, it has become increasingly possible for human beings to use one latent characteristic after another.

But it is also necessary to realize that characteristics that were used by human beings in earlier periods—or under very different conditions of living—may also have been mutilated or destroyed. In an over-all sense, genetic evolution led to the development of the human species. But there is no guarantee that henceforth the direction of human evolution will be safe or beneficent. Indeed, we know very well that evolution has very often taken disastrous bypaths in other species.

Therefore we have to consider very seriously the problem of our tremendously one-sided scientific development. For through this we may destroy ourselves and our planet as well. There is no guarantee—at least none that anthropologists have been able to find—that there is in human society an inherent capacity for self-preservation. Individuals, yes. Individuals have a capacity for self-preservation, but societies seem not to have. As we very well know, one civilization after another has collapsed, because its members lacked the power and the will to reorganize their way of life so that they could continue.

Until now the breakdown of older civilizations has not been desperately serious, because over time another people have taken over much of the culture and so very little of human knowledge was permanently lost. (This was not necessarily true, of course, of the cultures developed by very small groups of people; what was unique in such cultures inevitably was lost.) But today, in our interdependent world, given our present technical ability to destroy the whole planet, there is the very real possibility and danger that, lacking the societal capacity to take advantage of what we know to re-organize our life ways, we may actually destroy ourselves and all other living beings with us. This is the danger that confronts us.

Yet I believe that the more we can learn about the relationships between human culture, human learning and inherent human capacities, the better will be our chance to preserve and enhance life on this planet.

Two important things are in our favor. We now recognize that elements in our human nature include some that go back to the very beginning of life, to the time of plants, and some that have evolved through millions of years to produce mammals and primates and, among these, our own species. We also know that all human beings belong to one species, *Homo sapiens,* and that *Homo sapiens,* as we know our species, has not become appreciably differentiated in perhaps 20 thousand years. The smallest Pygmy and the Chinese sage with the largest head ever recorded are both members of our one species, and the capacity of any one human group to draw on this vast, complex human heritage is equal to that of any other large human group. Sometimes small, isolated societies have become too specialized to be able to draw fully on the human gene pool, but we have remained one species. So we have the whole human race to depend upon, providing we will put at the disposal of all societies all the knowledge we have gained and if we also become willing to draw on the accumulated cultural findings of different peoples in every part of the modern world.

This is what we mean when we say that today the West is learning from the East and, reciprocally, the East from the West. In time, the over-emphasis on certain aspects of life in the West may be balanced by a different emphasis on other aspects of life in the East. The Chinese ideogram has certain advantages, as well as certain disadvantages, as compared with our type of script. The use of our script has enormously developed our capacity for certain kinds of linear thinking, but at the same time it has made vastly difficult—or it has barred out —many kinds of circular thinking that are equally valuable. Our task now is to look at all these different capacities, wherever they have been developed in our own and in other very different cultures. Some are capacities that have appeared very fleetingly, possibly only in one society or a very long time ago; others may appear today among only a few peoples in the world.

Special talents and psychic gifts, as far as we know, are distributed throughout the earth, but they occur, we think, rather rarely. Now, making use of our highly developed capacity for invention, we may be able to actualize such talents in ways that were not guessed at earlier. For example, we may be able to keep alive kinds of individuals who, because they were so special and so fragile, have never before survived. And this, I think, is giving rise to new hope all over the world that certain unusual human capacities can be deliberately cultivated for the benefit of all human kind.

We know only too well that in any culture its members can make inventions that are dangerous as well as others that are beneficent. Warfare was such a dangerous invention. And once having invented the idea that members of a society could turn against their fellows in another society and, in so doing, treat them as somehow less than human or classify them as either predators or legitimate prey, human beings seemed unable to make the inventions necessary to free them from this entrapment in war. For we shall not rid ourselves of war until we find more viable ways of integrating the world's societies. What we face today is the fact that, temporarily or over many thousands of years, the course of human civilization as a whole has been deflected by one disastrous invention after another. And, unfortunately, we made the discovery of how to utilize nuclear energy at a time when we did not yet have the political or moral organization to deal with its immense potential for destruction. Thus there is the danger that we shall fasten on future generations a burden too great to bear or that we ourselves may at any moment destroy the entire planet. Had the world's peoples already achieved some form of viable, coherent and interconnected community before the development of nuclear power, we could perhaps have used this immense power for good and would not run the terrible risks that, today, we still are unwilling to acknowledge are real and ever present.

Yet I believe there is hope. For as we survey the course of
human civilization and the many ways in which, over time,
technical inventions have matched and complemented social
and political inventions, we realize that we have already opened
the way to a major change. Since the beginning of the indus-
trial revolution, almost everything has favored a giant scale—
everything has pointed to an economy of size and centraliza-
tion. Today this is being reversed. As we turn to the development of solar energy, we have an opportunity to develop a
technology that favors decentralization, localization, indigeni-
zation. For the first time in more than 150 years, a new technology can emphasize the unique qualities of each culture and
can permit us to move away from the dangers inherent in a
giant scale. This, in turn, may well facilitate more coherent
relationships between large and small societies.

But there is something else that may be equally important.
For thousands of years men have stood on the frontiers of their
land, where they have willingly fought and died—died to protect their women and children, died for their language and
religion, died to protect their land—a tiny patch or a great
nation—from those who would take it away. It has been very
difficult to imagine how any people might surmount the fixed
belief that if one group gained more territory, some other group
must have less and that no two individuals can stand in the
same spot, build a house or till a farm on the same piece of land.

Today, however, we have become aware of the air—that
natural element from which our greatest danger may come and
also our greatest good, our threats and all our good communication with one another. And, finally, we are discovering that
there are no frontiers in the air. Thus, for the first time in
human history, caring for our own and caring for the larger

whole can—and must—be treated as the same. Unless we care for our own family, our own city, our own country in ways that will protect our children from the dangers of pollution, we cannot protect the rest of the world. For the first time in human history the contrast between mine and thine—between protecting my own and protecting against others—is being removed. For the first time, technology—our ability to fly through the air, to send messages through the air, to send bombs through the air, to pollute the air all of us must breathe or to clear the air of pollution—seems to be moving toward the side of ongoing life and of protectedness.

As I see it there is hope in these two things. The decentralization and the relocalization that are made possible by the development of solar energy provide one kind of hope. The other hope is bound up with the recognition that because there are no frontiers in the air, the more we care for our children —all the earth's children—the more we shall protect the world, and the more we protect the whole world we live in, the more we can care for all our children.